The Public Professor

The Public Professor

Professor

How to Use Your Research to Change the World

M. V. LEE BADGETT

NEW YORK UNIVERSITY PRESS

New York and London

NEW YORK UNIVERSITY PRESS
New York and London
www.nyupress.org

References to Internet websites (URLs) were accurate at the time of writing. Neither the author nor New York University Press is responsible for URLs that may have expired or changed since the manuscript was prepared.

ISBN: 978-1-4798-1502-9 (hardback)
ISBN: 978-1-4798-6139-2 (paperback)

For Library of Congress Cataloging-in-Publication data, please contact the Library of Congress.

New York University Press books are printed on acid-free paper, and their binding materials are chosen for strength and durability. We strive to use environmentally responsible suppliers and materials to the greatest extent possible in publishing our books.

Manufactured in the United States of America

10 9 8 7 6 5 4 3 2 1

Also available as an ebook

To the activists, organizers, lawyers, politicians, protestors, funders, teachers, staffers, writers, and voters working to change the world, and the scholars working alongside them

Contents

Acknowledgments

During graduate school, I spoke to my parents every Sunday, and every Sunday they asked more or less the same question: "When are you going to start your dissertation?" Over the years that question morphed into, "When are you going to finish your dissertation, and what is it about again?" Answering that second question involved trying to make what I was studying real and relevant to them, which turned out to be excellent practice for a scholar who wanted to use her research to make a difference in the world.

The actual idea for this book was born after a series of discussions I organized at the Williams Institute for Sexual Orientation and Gender Identity Law and Public Policy at the UCLA School of Law in 2006–7. Gary Gates and I tried to figure out how to reverse engineer scholars like ourselves, and I wrote a "policy research manifesto" to teach young researchers how social science research could connect to policy debates about equality for lesbian, gay, bisexual, and transgender people. Those discussions created the foundation for the basic principles, strategies, and exercises outlined here to use for a much broader set of important social and environmental problems and issues.

The Williams Institute is a bridge between scholars and actual legal and policy debates, so it's been one important laboratory to develop my ideas about public engagement. I owe many thanks to my Williams Institute colleagues, to my colleagues at the Institute for Gay and Lesbian Strategic Studies (now merged with Williams), and to communication professionals I have worked with over the years. In particular, Aaron Belkin, Gary Gates, Ann Northrop, Jenny Pizer, Cathy Renna, Brad Sears, Scott Swenson, and Bob Witeck have been especially important colleagues whom I've been very grateful to learn about communication from and with.

My co-conspirators in developing the Public Engagement Project at UMass Amherst have also been amazingly supportive and inspiring sources of ideas for this book. The conversations I've had with Amy Schalet, Linda Tropp, Susan Newton, Wendy Varner, Maureen Perry-Jenkins, Naomi Gerstel, Lisa Troy, and Sally Powers have helped shape my thinking about engagement, and I thank them all profusely.

The participants at the panels and workshops we've put on together at UMass have provided valuable experiences and data that I've drawn on here. My Economics Department colleagues Nancy Folbre, Bob Pollin, and Jim Boyce have been excellent role models, as well as sources of wisdom. I am also grateful to the faculty, staff, and students at the Center for Public Policy and Administration, who have supported this project in many ways, as well. I also got to try out some of these ideas during a yearlong seminar sponsored by what is now the Interdisciplinary Studies Institute at UMass.

Scott Swenson generously agreed to co-author the social media chapter, and his energy, enthusiasm, and wisdom ended up transforming the whole book as a result. He might not have realized that decision also meant coaching me on Twitter, but I thank him for that, too.

One group I must thank by name are the generous people who've read drafts of these chapters and have given me helpful feedback at many different stages: Patricia Connelly, Naomi Gerstel, Michal Lumsden, Ide O'Carroll, Amy Schalet, Elizabeth Silver, Scott Swenson, and Bianca Wilson. Their suggestions made this a better book. I am also very grateful to three great role models, Teresa Ghilarducci, Stephanie Coontz, and Lisa Moore, all busy people who were willing to share their own professional experiences and knowledge with me. I tapped into my networks to pull together some of the advice presented in different chapters, and I thank Michael Crawford, Michael Lavers, Peter Montgomery, Susan Newton, Cathy Renna, and Brad Sears for sharing their practical knowledge. I'm also grateful to Luke Johnson and Avanti Mukherjee for their research assistance.

Ilene Kalish, my editor at NYU Press, deserves her own paragraph of thanks. She was surprised to hear that I wanted to write such a book, but she immediately got it and got behind the project. I'm thankful that she pushed me to keep improving this book and that she finally gave me a deadline.

I am profoundly grateful for the ongoing support of a small group of women whose wisdom, patience, and good instincts gave me the courage, motivation, and grounding to push on with this project. Randy Albelda shared her own experiences and ideas with me and is a wonderful role model. Lisa Moore got excited about the book and continues to remind me that engagement is a two-way street. Patricia Connelly took this project seriously and convinced me that there was something there to carry on with.

Finally, my wife, Elizabeth Silver, has always helped me to better understand what I was trying to do, and she patiently read many drafts and listened when I needed a sounding board. I am grateful for her wise and loving counsel. She had many more wonderful ideas and reactions than I could incorporate, and maybe that just means that there will be a sequel.

1

Speaking Truth to Empower
· · · · · · · · · · · · · · · · · · ·

As a kid, Gary Orfield read avidly about civil rights, a subject that seemed distant from his hometown of Minneapolis, which had few people of color in those days. When he was an undergraduate at the University of Minnesota in the early 1960s, university officials came to him with an unexpected request. "They asked me to figure out how to kind of orient and bring into college the American Indian students who were coming to our campus," Orfield recalled. He didn't know anything about American Indian students, though, other than that northern Minnesota had Indian reservations. So he organized a visit to those reservations, and eventually organized more trips for students to do projects. Those visits made a lasting impression on Orfield: "It made me realize how deep racism was, and how devastating it was."[1]

His interest in fighting racial injustice led Orfield to seek a career of research and action as a political scientist.[2] While in graduate school at the University of Chicago, he started going to school board meetings, and he eventually wrote a dissertation on the efforts to desegregate education and equalize opportunities in the South.

Over the five decades since then, Orfield has worked to make access to a high-quality education equal for all students. His research has explored a range of hotly contested means to that end: busing, school choice, No Child Left Behind, affirmative action, diversity, and fair housing. Orfield's research, as well as his understanding of politics and the educational system, landed him on commissions and in the expert witness box. Today he co-directs UCLA's Civil Rights Project, and his work is central to ongoing debates about the desegregation of school systems and to the Supreme Court's decisions on affirmative action in higher education.

Economist Teresa Ghilarducci never expected to be a policy entrepreneur. Her academic work and technical expertise in the obscure details of pensions landed her on many public and private pension and health care boards during a conventional academic career. However, now she finds herself promoting her idea for a new retirement plan for American workers to policymakers and the media.[3] "My identity was always as an academic bringing ideas to a mountain, to Congress," she explains. "What made me a policy entrepreneur is Rush Limbaugh and the right wing, when they started attacking me for being a communist."

Her third book put her on Limbaugh's radar. *When I'm Sixty-Four: The Plot against Pensions and the Plan to Save Them* laid out the plan for the Guaranteed Retirement Accounts (GRA) program. Workers would put 5% of their salary into their GRA, and they would get a tax credit of $600 (for example) to help pay for it. A public agency would manage the funds and guarantee a 2–4% return on savings after inflation, creating a new source of retirement income to add to Social Security. Limbaugh labeled this idea as socialist, but the *New York Times* recognized the GRA as one of the most innovative ideas of 2008. Today her idea is catching on with state legislators, as Ghilarducci explains to them about the crisis in retirement plans and how her GRA idea can make the lives of millions of older Americans more secure.

Historian Stephanie Coontz confesses that her transformation from scholar to public intellectual was largely accidental. Her first book took thirteen years to write and was as academic as it sounds: *The Social Origins of Private Life: A History of American Families.* "I was so concerned to prove myself to other academics that I wrote this ponderous book that often overwhelmed my storyline with data just to prove I had it and never used a dime word if I could dig a dollar one out of my pocket!" she laughingly admits now. By the time she finished the book, she noticed there was a new need for her knowledge: "I could take the research I had done and use it to counteract some of the myths that I was hearing, mostly from conservatives but also from liberals, about the past of the family."

Then she got lucky. In 1992, Coontz published a book on families for a popular audience called *The Way We Never Were.* Just as it came out, then vice president Dan Quayle ignited a raging public debate on "family values." Quayle criticized Murphy Brown, a fictional TV character played by Candice Bergen, for deciding to become a single mother, or as Quayle put it, "mocking the importance of fathers by bearing a child alone and calling it just another lifestyle choice."[4] The public uproar over family values might have been bad for society, Coontz points out, but it was timely for her, and she and her book publicists were ready: "That transformed me into the go-to person about whether it was really true that if we lived like the 1950s, we'd be better off."

Lisa D. Moore's best friend was diagnosed with AIDS in the 1980s, about the time she entered UC Berkeley's public health doctoral program. The HIV epidemic got more personal, and

Moore's commitment to research on HIV prevention intensi-
fied. For a course project, she studied San Francisco's Prevention
Point, one of the nation's first needle exchange programs. In an
act of civil disobedience, a group of anarchists, drug users, and
other activists had set up the illegal program to reduce HIV transmission by allowing injection drug users to trade used needles for
clean ones. Moore had to convince the anarchists that a researcher
had something to contribute to the cause. Her study eventually
demonstrated the value of Prevention Point and the commitment
of the drug users in the program to preventing HIV.

After her course was over, Moore continued to work with the
group to educate skeptical local policymakers and the African
American community about the need to adopt a legal, better-
funded program. Would this program work? Would it increase
drug use? Moore's role was to translate findings from her own research and that of other scholars to show that needle exchange
programs could reduce HIV transmission without exacerbating
drug use. A few years later, the city decided to fund the program,
and it eventually became legal.

The work Moore did with needle exchanges after that first study
was central to her development as a teacher, scholar, and community activist. She began to view drug users as agents in their own
lives and, as she puts it, "to see how they are actively in their own
way trying to make things better." Having such street knowledge
is important when her scholarly role gives her a privileged position in policy discussions. "No people in policy debates are poor
street-based drug users," Moore points out. "But that's why it's
important to have some representation of what [street-based drug
users] need."

I've been lucky to encounter these four very different scholars—
call them public intellectuals, scholar activists, "pracademics," or

engaged scholars—either in person or on the page. Their stories line up with my own trajectory as an academic: seeing an injustice, studying that problem, wanting to make a difference, injecting scholarship into important public debates, taking advantage of good timing, being willing to handle disagreement, and enjoying the engagement with policymakers, activists, and the public outside of the university. We've learned more about the worlds we study as our engagement has taken us into unfamiliar settings and brought us unexpected challenges.

I will never forget the first time I testified before Congress. The impressive looking invitation that I received from a congressional committee chair included a polite but firm request that oral testimony be limited to five minutes. A little box on the witness table flashes green, yellow, and red lights to give committee witnesses a familiar reminder when their time is almost up.

Reducing years of detailed economic research into five minutes of respectfully persuasive and informative content was a daunting task. Looking up into the eyes of distinguished lawmakers as I spoke the words that I had rehearsed made the work worthwhile, though. The opportunity to speak directly to them was both a great privilege and a daunting responsibility that I had been eagerly seeking for fifteen years.

One of my earliest research studies convincingly (in my view) debunked the myth of gay affluence. Opponents of gay civil rights laws routinely point to the allegedly privileged economic position of lesbian, gay, and bisexual people to argue they don't need legal protections against discrimination. My research shows that view is wrong—they are not a high-earning elite, and gay and bisexual men actually earn *less* than similarly qualified heterosexual men. Discrimination characterizes gay workers' experiences, not privilege.

The moment I read my first statistical printouts with these findings I was ready to speak this new truth to our nation's lawmakers. For a long time, though, I watched from the sidelines as advocates on one side skillfully used the worst economic stereotypes of gay people, while advocates on the other side did little to counter them. How could I directly transmit my important knowledge to powerful decision makers, who surely just needed to hear the facts so they could pass the right policy?

Once the first call finally came, I learned more about how I got there. I started to see how other scholars might get to the point of speaking truth to power—or speaking the truth to empower—just as Orfield, Ghilarducci, Coontz, and Moore have.

My job for more than two decades has been to be an economics and public policy professor, so I've had an insider's view of how professors see our role, which rarely extends beyond academia. As scholars, we live and die (professionally, anyway) through our capacity to reason and persuade our colleagues. We have professional norms and customs to guide our research. We have our students to take our wisdom and insights from the classroom into the "real world." University evaluation procedures keep us on a professionally productive path of research and publications. We get rewards of status, sabbaticals, and raises for staying professionally active. All of these features of academic life focus our attention on one key audience—ourselves.

And that all works for us, at least until the day comes that we want someone outside of our academic worlds to listen to us because we know something important:

- We've discovered some new problem that no one has been paying much attention to.

- We see an injustice that can be righted.
- We've got a good idea for how to address or even solve some social problem.
- We hear about a policymaker or public figure who's just gotten a fact or judgment terribly wrong.
- We think a public debate is missing the point on some issue of the day.
- We've got good advice for individuals about how to improve their mental health, physical well-being, or economic status.

I have many smart colleagues who've got something to teach the world outside the university but don't know the answer to a key question: How do we get policymakers, the media, and community members to pay attention to us?

It's not just our own personal sense of social usefulness or professional pride that's at stake here. We live in an era of declining public support for higher education and increasing public doubts about the value of scientific knowledge. If we can grab the public's attention and make research relevant and accessible, we might increase their enthusiasm for supporting public higher education.

Most of us are ourselves products of the publicly supported higher education system, so we have even more of a responsibility to connect knowledge to the public interest. Many of us borrowed money, got parental support, or received public funding that put us through college and graduate school. I would argue that we have our own debt to society to pay.

The good news is that paying that debt back by sharing our knowledge with the broader world is also personally and professionally rewarding. It's not just about feeling useful, since we can learn much more about the world we study when we play a broader part in it. Many other professors have gotten new research questions, new perspectives, new ideas, new sources of data, and occasionally even new funding opportunities by interacting with the broader public. That can all add up to better research as well as even more engagement.

The bad news? There really isn't any, but figuring out how to be effective in public discussions as academics requires a little more knowledge, some commitment of time, and a few additional skills. Most of us aren't equipped to move from dissertation writer to public intellectual or publicly engaged scholar without learning about how to do that.

Sure, you can probably name a scholar in your field whose academic work attracted the attention of some powerful person who pulled that professor out of scholarly obscurity and into a prominent public position. But my educated guess is that in 99% of those situations, that academic overnight sensation had already developed both a personal network that included important people and a set of communication skills that set him or her up for success and influence. Academics don't end up on NPR or the *PBS NewsHour*, at the White House, or in front of lawmakers by accident or blind luck.

Making a difference by engaging in the public conversation or debate about the issues that your work addresses isn't a matter of stumbling onto fame and fortune—it's a matter of being effective and strategic, and this book is designed to help you develop the strategy and skills you need.

My own road to the congressional witness chair began with the education in policymaking that I got as a student activist in high school and college, working on local politicians' campaigns and other causes. I decided to get a Ph.D. in economics so that I could better understand and influence policies that addressed problems like discrimination and unemployment. As a graduate student, I got practice by using my writing and analytical skills in campus debates about graduate student unions, affirmative action in education, and equal access to faculty jobs for women and people of color.

With a completed dissertation in hand, my first job at a school of public policy in the Washington, D.C., area opened up new types of engagement and expanded my personal network of people who are professionally engaged in the policy process. Policymakers, lawyers, community groups, employers, and others involved in the political process who learned about my research encouraged me to weigh in with an "expert's" view on employment discrimination in the open hearings in state legislatures and other contexts.

I eventually learned that congressional hearings have not only more gravitas, but also a carefully choreographed lineup of witnesses, determined mostly by the majority party. Unlike more open processes in state legislatures, for Congress it's "No invitation, no in-person testimony." When the time came for me, the real invitation was not in a letter, but in the phone call from a committee staffer to vet me for my availability, accessibility, and appropriateness. That staffer in turn, had tapped into his network, speaking with knowledgeable insiders, advocacy organization staffs, and other experts to come up with my name as someone who could provide useful testimony.

Of course, the academic research and analysis that I had conducted over many years clearly had something to do with the invitation. Equally important was the *other* work I have done to create and feed that professional network that extends beyond my fellow academics and includes the people making decisions about hearing witnesses.

Over the last two decades, I've answered reporters' phone calls, consulted with attorneys and policymakers' staffs, followed up on businesses' requests for information, written op-eds, attended community meetings, talked with activists, listened to the arguments of participants in debates, provided memos and briefings to different stakeholders, provided summaries of academic work on different topics, been an expert witness in court cases, participated in webinars, submitted blog posts, tweeted study findings, and cranked out scores of policy reports. I've participated in the development of two think tanks to build an institutional publication and communications capacity on sexual orientation– and gender identity–related public policy issues. Those activities weren't a means to an end—they have been much more important in my own engaged life than the more glamorous congressional hearing.

If I were starting this work today, I suspect that new social media would take up a bigger chunk of space on that list of activities. Even as someone with a rather old-fashioned attachment to direct face-to-face interaction, I've promoted a book with a Facebook page, participated in online book chats, taught an online course, built a small Twitter following, guest blogged on several sites, and published online essays. These new media opportunities have enhanced the power of my networks for getting my research findings into the hands of people who need them—a power that I will have you tapping into later on, too.

Certainly my level of involvement in the policy process puts me on the extremely active end of the engagement spectrum, but I've seen many valuable public contributions by academics who are less intensively involved, too. Every day I hear about research produced by my colleagues that has the as-yet untapped potential to improve the world. Many of them want to bridge the gap between their work and the "real world" but don't know how to begin:

- senior colleagues who've reached a point in their careers that gives them the knowledge and opportunity to reach out beyond academia but who don't know how to connect to policy debates;
- young scholars fresh out of Ph.D. programs and eager to change the world who've come face-to-face with the more urgent demand to publish or perish;
- media-savvy colleagues who still find it hard to actively influence public debates;
- mid-career friends who are ready to engage but don't see how they could find time in busy career and family schedules to develop influence;
- idealistic graduate students who went back to school to enhance their ability to contribute to social change but are disillusioned by the culture and incentive systems in academic life.

How can we make meaningful and influential connections in community and policy work? To answer that question, I have talked with my colleagues at UMass Amherst and at UCLA's Williams Institute, one of the think tanks I worked to develop, along with other influential scholars. I've tried to "reverse engineer" our own lives and career paths to identify what we have learned that would help our colleagues, post-docs, and graduate students get where we are more quickly. This book flows primarily from those experiences and conversations, along with a few lessons from relevant research.

Box 1.1. Examples of How to Use Research to Make a Difference

- Team up with a social movement or community organization to design a research project
- Evaluate an existing approach to addressing a problem
- Talk to a journalist about the public relevance of new research you've published
- Present research findings at hearings of city councils, state legislatures, or Congress
- Tweet about the lessons from research that apply to an issue in the headlines
- Write an op-ed about a problem that needs to be thought of in a different way
- Speak to a local organization about research (yours and others) and how it might apply to the organization's work
- Write a letter to an agency head to let them know about recent research that is related to the agency's mission
- Brief a policymaker about a problem that they can do something about
- Serve on a board or commission for an organization or policy-making body

My goal in this book is to provide tools and knowledge to help you, a new or experienced scholar, connect your research and ideas with people and institutions outside of the academy in order to influence a situation that matters to you.

In my experience and from my observations of influential academics like the ones I've introduced in this chapter, three pieces are essential for making that happen: understanding the big picture, learning to communicate with new audiences, and building a broad network. This book pulls those three elements apart to understand why each is important and to provide practical suggestions for how to accomplish each goal.

1. *See the big picture: the terms of the debate and the rules of the game.* Behind almost any meaningful issue is a public conversation that involves some disagreement. Understanding the whole debate, discussed in chapter 2, helps you find an effective entry point on an issue via your own research and ideas. You'll also see what else you need to know, since we often need to explain the big picture, not just our own relatively narrow slice of knowledge. Connecting knowledge to change also means understanding the rules of the game in relevant decision-making contexts outlined in chapter 3, such as legislatures or courts, and who the influential actors in the public debate are.

2. *Build a network of relationships that extends into the work and institutions you hope to influence.* The old adage for finding a job works here, too: *It's not what you know, it's who you know.* And you need to be proactive to build that network. Chapter 3 provides the first step in this process: identifying the players in the larger web of action on your issue so that you can strategically build your own network. Chapter 4 discusses how to build a rich professional network that extends well beyond academia to include journalists, policymakers and their staffs, community organizations, or others who provide the connections you'll need. Once your network understands how your knowledge and research matters in the context they work in, those individuals take your ideas into important places that you can't go.

3. *You need to know how to communicate ideas to people who aren't in your field.* Anyone who has tried to explain their research to a nonacademic friend or relative discovers how comfortable we are with our disciplinary shorthand and how hard it is to push beyond that. Those of us who are teachers already

work with an audience outside of our field—our students. We can also learn to use new genres that appeal to a wider range of audiences through blogs, tweets, newspapers, radio shows, or briefing papers. Chapters 5–7 provide nuts-and-bolts tips on how to communicate effectively in many different contexts.

But effective communication involves more than communicating clearly at an appropriate level in new formats. Debates take place on many levels, sometimes seemingly rational and academic sounding, but more often involving "frames" that tap into emotions and deeply rooted ways of seeing the world that people are not always aware of. Being persuasive and influential in that context means understanding and making the most of—or maybe even challenging—the dominant frames on an issue. Chapter 5 starts the discussion of communication with some general lessons about messages, talking points, and framing. Chapters 6 and 7 provide more detailed advice on using traditional media and new social media to get your knowledge into the world.

The last two chapters address additional challenges. Every now and then a scholar will find herself in the middle of an uncomfortably hot debate that gets personal. Chapter 8 addresses ways of preventing and dealing with those heated moments. The common challenge that all of us face, though, is how to make time for public engagement in an already busy life. Chapter 9 offers some strategies for managing time and for getting around the false trade-off of engagement vs. research time. Engagement can enhance your teaching and research and can even help you get tenure and promotion with some planning.

No matter what form your engagement takes, the big three points will provide a strong base for engaging in the public conversation. You could read this as a how-to guide for fruitful engagement as a scholar if you're just starting down that path. For researchers who have already started down the road, the book offers a chance to find some new places and ways to engage more effectively.

The form that engagement takes and the goals you pursue are up to you. You might want to position yourself to speak as an "expert" who has knowledge relevant for decision makers in some policy context. You might work intensively for many years with a local organization that wants to better understand the roots of a community problem through research. You might also become a scholar-activist, working for a cause that is related to the subject of your research. You might even become a public intellectual, creating a well-read blog, amassing Twitter followers, or being asked to speak up in public contexts on different issues of the day, whether directly connected to your own research or some larger intellectual issues. No matter which direction you want to go, this book will help you lay out a path to use your research to change the world.

A Call to Scholarly Engagement

The world faces grave problems: disruptive climate change, persistent social and economic inequality, ongoing armed conflicts, threats to democracy, and infrastructure meltdowns, among others. These global problems have parallels and impacts at the national, state, and local levels in the United States. In the face of these daunting global and local challenges and in the context of our own busy careers, it's tempting to keep our heads in our books and computers, hoping that our students and published ideas will trickle down from the ivory tower into the world to make a difference.

I believe that giving in to that temptation would be a lost opportunity and an abdication of our social responsibility.

In 2014, *New York Times* columnist Nicholas Kristof made a similar plea: "Professors, we need you!"[5] He claimed that most academics "just don't matter in today's great debates" and called on us to change our "culture of exclusivity." Kristof's column upset many scholars, who pushed back, pointing out that many professors engage on public matters through their blogs, outreach to policymakers, and teaching.[6] Conversations about public sociology and public anthropology, for example, show that many scholars value public engagement. But these academics also pointed out their heavy workloads, the lack of support for engagement, and the decline of tenure-track jobs, all of which make public involvement difficult.

I sympathize with both sides. While I acknowledge the existence of those challenges, I also think that more of us can become actively engaged, and most importantly, we can all become more effective in ways that improve—not threaten—our teaching, research, and professional reputations. Thomas Piketty's breakthrough work on income inequality, Cornel West's insights into racial justice, and Elizabeth Warren's path from the classroom to the Senate all show us that scholars can engage and can make an impact, and you'll meet more scholars like them in this book.

I'm not arguing that scholars have all the answers and deserve the world's undivided attention and allegiance. We don't. In a democracy, our elected representatives, fellow voters, and professional academics will discuss problems, debate solutions, and make decisions based on a political process, not the dictates of an intelligentsia and their applications of reason and rationality. In academia, we will continue to study and debate our findings, methods, and theories in intricate detail and in our own scholarly lingo. But surely we have *something* useful to contribute to public discussions and debates about social, cultural, economic, scientific, and political issues, big and small.

"Decisions must be made," Gary Orfield wisely notes, "so the question becomes whether intellectuals should engage in presenting the best available evidence or should simply abstain, letting obviously important decisions be made on the basis of prejudice or anecdote. My choice has been to be engaged."[7]

Engagement is also not a matter of left vs. right. The stereotype about liberal professors has some basis in fact. I'm certainly one of them. But effective public engagement on important issues is not limited to one point or another of the political spectrum. In fact, I've gotten a lot of great ideas about engagement by studying the practices of conservative scholars and think tanks.

Our public debates benefit from having many different viewpoints represented. As academics, we should be role models for passionate but thoughtful debates, using facts and complex ideas instead of sound bites. We can model agreeing to disagree without being disagreeable, as the saying goes. Teresa Ghilarducci points to scholars' biggest assets in the public realm: "Our public engagement effectiveness comes from trust that comes from good research. . . . We have students, and we have an expectation that we know both sides."

Your work can matter, and you can be influential at a public level. But the path to becoming a public professor, influential policy advisor, scholar-activist, valued community resource, or go-to person on an issue is not one that we're trained to walk as scholars. Using this book to repurpose what you already know about how the world works plus acquiring a few new skills will position you for *engagement*—being involved and hoping to make a difference—and for *impact*—actually making a difference.

Box 1.2. Five Easy Ways to Get Started

1. Send a letter to the editor of a newspaper in response to an article related to your research
2. Post articles and tweet comments related to your research area on Facebook and Twitter
3. Write a press release for your next academic publication
4. Contact your university news office to get on their list of faculty experts
5. Find opportunities to meet your state representatives and member of Congress

2

Seeing the Big Picture, Part 1
· · · · · · · · · · · · · · · · · · · ·
Understanding the Debate

When scholars want to make change in the world, the first big step is to figure out how and where we can be useful. Teresa Ghilarducci apprenticed in public engagement when she was studying labor economics in grad school—she just didn't know it at the time. She had a job working with labor unions preparing for bargaining sessions, so she got to see theory in action and learned about the labor market from the inside. Over the years she learned the practical details about retirement issues and pensions. She learned what the important questions were, and when pensions and retirement policy hit the headlines, she was ready.

Daniel Gade has a doctorate in public policy and studies health policy for veterans, but his apprenticeship was a little different.[1] As a tank company commander in Iraq, he lost a leg and spent a year recovering. His next stop was the White House, where he advised President George W. Bush on health care and disability policy for veterans and active service members. Lieutenant Colonel Gade now puts his knowledge about veterans to work with his West Point students and in the policy world. He argues that veterans' cash disability benefits are a disincentive to work, and veterans would be better served—and healthier and more socially integrated—with a program that rewarded them directly for working. As the number of recipients and cost of veterans' disability benefits rises, his idea is getting more attention, both positive and negative, from veterans, policymakers, journalists, and funders.

Both Ghilarducci and Gade *have developed a view of the big picture*, a key practice for scholars who want to fit into public life. What their experiences have in common is that they got into a big, seemingly chaotic, public debate and found a place in it. Finding the "you are here" point in some debate is a first step for anyone who wants to be an effective and engaged scholar.

Games—whether soccer, chess, or a formal debate—are a good metaphor for the world of public involvement. Sometimes these debates are real contests with winners and losers. I have occasionally felt like a gladiator, although not in an ugly fight to the death, fortunately. And it's more like football than tennis, since engagement is a team activity, with you playing a particular position on the field.

Engagement also feels like playing an actor's role. We might be heroes in some stories, and bit players in others. For now, don't worry about what your role will be. In this chapter, we'll figure out how to get an overview of the contest and develop some tools to find our way around the playing field.

Locate the Debate

Do scholars know how to argue? It's practically a job requirement. You're probably already part of a *scholarly* debate about something, with competing interpretations and explanations of patterns observed in the data or texts you study. Debate is often how we expand knowledge and understanding. That training in responding to disagreement with reasoned arguments and in changing your own mind will come in handy in the public arena.

However, the question that the public cares about will probably not be posed in the same way as an academic question. The public questions generally involve a "should" of some kind, even if it's just implied:

- Should we raise taxes to increase funding for public education?
- Should we increase regulation of the food industry to promote greater food safety?
- Should we regulate the sale of guns?
- Should we require labeling of genetically modified foods?
- How should we organize our health care system?

For example, a big question motivating labor economics asks why people get paid what they do. Of course, we have different theories and a lively debate about who gets what and why. It's a very short step from that big theoretical question in academia to big questions in the public arena: Why do men get paid more than women, and what should we do about that? Can we raise the minimum wage without destroying jobs? How should we address rising income and wealth inequality? Should we regulate CEOs' pay if they get paid more than they're worth?

At this point, I assume that you've got some idea about the issues or decisions that you want to influence. You might even have a picture in mind of the relevant decision makers and situations that you'll focus on, whether it involves a judge, Congress, a particular business, or some social movement organization. You might already know where you can fit in. But if not, or if you think you're being underutilized, the rest of this chapter presents some exercises and perspectives that will help you find a path from point A, your participation in an academic conversation about a topic, to point B, your role in a public conversation or debate.

Taking Sides?

True confession: I was on my high school debate team and loved the competitive thrill of a structured debate with a judge who decided which team made the best case. Even if you don't think of yourself as a competitor, the fact that you care deeply enough to want to influence a public conversation suggests that you want to see social change or some particular outcome. If you can see the different sides in a public debate, then you can identify the teams in the contest. If you can see those teams' strategies and tactics in getting to an outcome, then you're on the way to finding your role in some part of that debate.

One concern that scholars might feel is that public engagement is partisanship or advocacy in a competitive context. But you don't have to take one side or argue a position in the same way forever. (In high school debate, we had to be ready to argue both sides of the issue.) Much valuable engagement by scholars is not about taking sides. Stephanie Coontz's engagement led her to co-found the Council on Contemporary Families, an organization that is publicly engaged but does not take positions on policy issues or candidates.

And you never know who your allies might turn out to be. Sociologist Sara Goldrick-Rab's own views tend toward the very liberal end of the spectrum, but she has worked with self-identified conservatives in her efforts to translate her research on college affordability into action by policymakers and the financial aid world.[2]

The main point here, though, is that other players in the debate are taking sides on the issue that you're interested in, and the impact of your involvement will depend on how you fit into the overall context. If you want to manage how your ideas are interpreted and incorporated into the debate—even if your involvement is talking to journalists about research findings or in presenting your work outside of more partisan contexts—you need to understand the game and play your position in it well.

Getting into the Game

If you were learning a new game, seeing where it takes place and reading a rulebook would give you very little sense of how to go out and actually play it, much less play it well. The next chapter will take you through some rules and into the arena. But you'll learn faster if you watch for a bit to see the big picture and get a feel for how it works.

Meet the people you'll engage with when you start engaging in the debate. Box 2.1 suggests some opportunities to see those folks in action. If you're lucky, you might stumble on a real old-fashioned debate on your issue of interest in print, online, or in person. For instance, the *New York Times* has frequent online debates on a wide variety of issues in the news ("Room for Debate," www.nytimes.com/roomfordebate). Less frequently, *The Economist* has something similar where readers can vote and participate (www.economist.com/debate/archive). More likely you'll want to piece together your own sense of the perspectives represented in many different contexts. If the issue is a high-profile one, you'll also start to recognize the real people involved who are influencing and leading the debate.

Box 2.1. Find the Debate

Things to read:

- News coverage and press releases
- Op-ed pieces and editorials
- Blogs written by organizations and other partisans on all sides
- Scholarly articles (especially in law journals) laying out the debate on an issue
- Friend-of-the-court briefs (amicus curiae briefs)
- Official court filings and briefs from litigants
- Transcripts of congressional hearings published in the *Congressional Record*
- Text of state and federal bills (see www.thomas.gov for congressional bill text and status; start with the website for your state legislature for state-specific bills)

Things to watch or listen to:

- Congressional hearings on C-SPAN
- TV shows that involve give and take on issues, like *PBS NewsHour*, or MSNBC and Fox News Channel pundit shows (think O'Reilly, Maddow, Hannity)
- Talk radio (you want a show that allows some give and take, although the one-sided ones might be useful, too.)

Some Simple Tools for Understanding the Debate

My basic assumption here is that you're interested in a contentious issue. I'll also assume that you care enough about that issue to already know something—maybe even a lot—about the arguments offered in the debate about it. You probably have some answers to questions like these: Is raising taxes to provide more funding for public higher education a good investment? Will greater regulation of food, the environment, or financial institutions inhibit businesses from creating jobs and shareholder profits? How much do we need to reduce greenhouse gas emissions?

Chances are good that your first instinct in answering those questions or others more relevant to you is to draw on your knowledge of that issue and the analytical tools used in your discipline. And if you've followed the debate in the kind of contexts listed in Box 2.1, you might have lots of potential answers. Your first step, though, is to figure out whether you can answer *important* questions in the debate.

Take a step back for a few minutes to look at the bigger picture in your debate. Getting the big picture means (1) seeing the different facets of the debate in context, (2) understanding the arguments put forward by participants, and (3) digging down to see the underlying assumptions, framings, and contexts that structure the debate. Once you've sketched out that picture, you can identify potential places for you and your research to make a difference. Hopefully, one of those places will show you where you can plug yourself into the debate.

What's the Question?

First, try to identify more specifically the questions that people are debating that are related to your areas of knowledge and interest. One way to think about this is to identify the changes in some behavior, policy, institution, or situation that someone is considering or to identify the problem that's a subject of a public discussion.

In the real world, the debate can look like one issue but might involve several different questions. It's helpful to identify all of those questions that you can, even when they circle some broader version of what you see as the central question.

For example, in recent years we've seen growing concerns about killings of unarmed black men by police officers. A public uproar swept the country in 2014 when Michael Brown, a young unarmed resident of Ferguson, Missouri, was shot by a police officer, and the uproar spilled over into nationwide protests when that officer was not indicted for a crime. The national discussion generated lots of questions. Is the problem the police—their training, their military equipment, their unconscious biases? Or did the problem become unruly and destructive protesters? Should we put special prosecutors in charge when a police officer kills someone? If we made changes that led to improved voter turnout and engagement, would municipal governments and police departments become more responsive to the African American community's concerns? Or are such tragedies inevitable without extensive reform of the entire criminal justice system? Scholars continue to debate these questions in newspapers, television shows, public events, and social media.

Questions in the climate change debate have ranged from the state of scientific evidence to the wisdom of free vs. regulated markets. Context and personal positions will influence how someone would ask the question, and the answers and even the debate are likely to be different, depending on how the question is posed.

Identify the Arguments

Once you have a handle on the questions guiding the debate, jump into the arguments. One crude but sometimes helpful way to start is to brainstorm the pros and cons. On one side of a piece of paper, list the arguments made by proponents of the issue; on the other side, list the arguments raised by opponents. You can get fancier and line up the pros and cons that respond to the other side, too.

To give you a detailed example of how this works, I'll use an issue that I've deeply explored from many different angles: Should we allow same-sex couples to marry? Box 2.2 lists issues in this long-running debate, a debate that has benefited greatly from scholar involvement.

Err on the side of listing every argument that pops into your head, and write all the variations down—not just the ones that you think have some merit, and not just the ones that are based on good reasons. You can go back later and cull, combine, or organize them.

Another practice that is both strategically helpful as well as ethically appropriate in debates is one that philosophers often advocate—generosity. Stephanie Coontz sees this as important both for communication and for getting the benefits of engagement in our scholarship. "I think it's made my research more complex because I've had to listen to people that I would normally dismiss as nonintellectual, non–research based, or maybe even nuts," Coontz argues. "You've got to figure out what is the kernel of truth or at least what are the real things that they're talking to? Have they raised arguments that really do force you to modify your position?" Even if those challenges don't lead Coontz to modify her position, she works on her own arguments to win her opponents over, or at least to get them to hear her argument more clearly. Coontz reports one big positive effect from her willingness to hear counterarguments clearly and generously: "I think it's made my research better and my teaching better."

So put forward the best possible version of an argument, even if you rarely hear it and especially if you disagree with it. You'll be better prepared for responding to and incorporating a particular argument in all its guises, plus you'll look like a more reasonable debater if you find yourself in that kind of context. I also think this practice is important for having productive and civil public debates—it's no guarantee, but it can't hurt.

Box 2.2. Example: Brainstorming Pros and Cons of Gay Marriage

PRO	CON
All individuals should have the same right to marry the person of their choice, whether that person is a man or a woman.	Marriage has evolved to accommodate the needs of different-sex couples, since men and women have different needs. Same-sex couples' needs might be very different.
Same-sex couples (SSCs) want to marry to express their love and commitment to each other, just as different-sex couples do.	Marriage is primarily a religious ritual, and the state should not dictate a change that violates the beliefs of all religious traditions.
SSCs and their children would benefit economically and psychologically from the legal and economic security provided by or enhanced by marriage.	The state should not force faith-based communities or organizations to recognize a relationship that violates their moral beliefs.
SSCs are deprived of important legal and economic benefits of marriage.	Most people do not think gay couples should have the right to marry, so the public should have the right to vote down gay marriage, even if legislatures or judges want to impose it.
Excluding SSCs from marriage leads to "minority stress" that is harmful to the physical and mental health of LGBT people.	Different-sex couples are the most likely to need access to marriage since they are much more likely to have children than are same-sex couples.
State governments benefit from lower spending in providing things that married couples provide each other, e.g., income support and health insurance.	Children do best when raised by different-sex parents.

Box 2.2. Example: Brainstorming Pros and Cons of Gay Marriage (*cont.*)

PRO	CON
Businesses would benefit from allowing SSCs to marry, both through spending on weddings and by having LGBT employees who feel more equal.	Many same-sex couples have chosen not to marry when they've had the opportunity, suggesting a low demand for marriage. In fact, some LGBT people oppose the political effort to win the right to marry within the LGBT community.
Providing a separate legal status instead of marriage stigmatizes gay relationships and creates a formal second-class status for those relationships.	Same-sex couples should be given some of the rights and benefits of marriage in a separate legal status.
	Allowing same-sex couples to marry could change the institution of marriage in ways that would harm marriage and heterosexual couples' families. For instance, if same-sex couples are less stable, the expectation of lifelong marriage will become even more jeopardized, perhaps destabilizing the marriages of heterosexual couples.
	Parents will lose control of what their children are taught in school about homosexuality and gay marriage, even when those teachings conflict with parents' values.

See the Debate Content

To get a better understanding of the strengths of the arguments that you identify, you can deepen your understanding with a scorecard-like tool that debate teams have used over the years, what they call a "flow chart." Start with the arguments for one side of the argument, pro or con. Draw an arrow from each argument to the response offered by the other side. That answer might be one of the other arguments. Then think about the response to the response; draw another arrow to that second response. Repeat as necessary. Box 2.3 shows two examples of how to reorganize the same-sex marriage debate from Box 2.2. What you'll have at the end is a sense of what an actual live debate between two or more people about this topic could look like. You'll probably also see some holes where you don't know a response to an argument, or where there has been no response offered.

Let's look at a real debate on a heated topic: genetically engineered organisms (or GMO). You can see part of the flow chart (Box 2.4) I created from a debate between plant geneticist and GMO pioneer Pamela Ronald and two GMO skeptics, journalist Michael Pollan and activist Raj Patel.[3] Ronald has a "take no prisoners" reputation among GMO critics, and she has shown herself to be a formidable debater in print.[4] She's got the scientific knowledge and a broad contextual understanding of the social costs and benefits of genetic engineering, and she comes across as personable and thoughtful on stage. Pollan and Patel are articulate, well-informed writers and participants in the world of food activism.

With the generosity of good debaters and the willingness to listen carefully, the three managed to find much common ground. All three want to reduce the amount of harmful chemicals used

Box 2.3. Flow Chart with Gay Marriage Argument Examples

Argument	Counterargument	Counter-counterargument
PRO Gay Marriage		
Same-sex couples are deprived of important legal and economic benefits of marriage.	These benefits are related to having children, so same-sex couples don't need them.	Many same-sex couples are raising children and need those benefits.
	We can give same-sex couples those benefits through an alternative status, like civil unions.	A separate status stigmatizes gay relationships and creates a second-class status.
AGAINST Gay Marriage		
Marriage is primarily a religious ritual, and the state should not dictate a change that violates the beliefs of all religious traditions.	Laws must support rational government purposes, not religious beliefs. No faith would be required to conduct same-sex weddings.	Business owners (like photographers or florists) whose religious beliefs conflict with homosexuality might be forced to serve gay couples.
	Some religious denominations are willing to perform weddings for same-sex couples but cannot.	The vast majority of religious traditions do not recognize same-sex relationships.

Box 2.4. Flow Chart of Examples from the GMO Debate

Argument	Counterargument	Counter-counterargument
PRO GMO		
The introduction of genetically engineered crops has big benefits, such as greatly reducing farmers' use of toxic pesticides.	But farming GMO crops has also led to weeds resistant to the pesticides designed for use with GMO crops, so more harmful pesticides are used.	Weeds are always a problem for farmers, and genetically modified seed won't solve them all. Farmers should use integrated pest management techniques like crop rotation and refuges.
Genetically modified seed generates higher yields, increasing the food supply without needing to farm more land.	In some countries, farmers report that yields have fallen after using the GMO seeds for a while.	No direct response
AGAINST GMO		
Genetically engineered foods are lightly regulated.	Many riskier ways of genetically modifying foods are considered safe and are even certified organic, like mutagenesis (radiation), and are less regulated.	We do regulate things like additives, for example. The choice of what gets regulated is a political decision.

Box 2.4. Flow Chart of Examples from the GMO Debate (*cont.*)

Argument	Counterargument	Counter-counterargument
AGAINST GMO		
The safety of genetically engineered foods has not been proven.	You have to assess safety on a case-by-case basis. Respected scientific organizations that have reviewed evidence on existing products say they are safe. You can't guarantee that a food is safe. All foods come with risks, including those related to use of herbicides, and generation of pollution. Those other risks are less with GMO foods.	We need more studies.
Genetic engineering has concentrated power in the food system for corporations that develop the GMO seeds and just want to make money.	Some genetically engineered crops were developed without the profit motive, through research in universities funded by government agencies and foundations, so farmers don't face the same access problems.	But the vast majority of the GMO crops used now are products of a few companies.

in farming. Pollan sees the value of genetic engineering that saved papayas from a virus in Hawaii. Ronald supports the kind of integrated pest management that organic farmers use, and she agrees that GMO products should be created and distributed by organizations without a profit motive. Ronald is more confident about scientific evidence of the safety of GMO foods than either Patel or Pollan, though. In spite of their remaining disagreements, creating a flow chart helped at least one virtual audience member (me) better understand where hard questions remain.[5]

Finding a Role: Assess the State of the Debate

As a scholar who wants to be part of the debate, your job is different from the debater preparing to argue all points on both sides.[6] You want to figure out how you will fit in and what your role will be in this particular debate. Two paths into the debate flow from this point, and both are productive in different ways.

The first path basically involves assessing the role of ideas and the quality of the thinking in the debate so far. Here are some (admittedly overlapping) questions to ask about your scorecard or flow chart that might lead you in useful directions:

- How strong are the arguments that you see in the debate?
- Are there counterarguments for each of the main arguments for each side?
- How strong are the sources of support for each argument and counterargument?
- Which aspects of the debate appeal to reason and which ones appeal to morality or emotion?
- What assumptions about the world underlie each argument?
- How are these arguments framed and why?

- How persuasive are the arguments that you see in the debate? Why are they persuasive? Who would find them persuasive?
- In which decision-making contexts do those arguments work best or are they most appropriate to use?
- How much of the debate is about the process of how an issue will be decided and who gets to decide, e.g., voters, judges, or legislators?
- Where are the holes or missing counterarguments?

In the course of thinking through those questions, you might see many opportunities for a scholar to contribute ideas and lessons from research. Sometimes even the process of evaluation itself is a useful exercise, and if you write up your thoughts on the subject, you've got something of use for people in the middle of the debate who would appreciate an outsider's view.

A Different Path: Targeting Research to Assess Consequences

This first path—casting a critical eye on a debate—is a classic academic exercise. The second path, emphasizing the more targeted use of research, might be a view into somewhat less familiar territory. On one level, understanding the role of research could be as simple as evaluating the quality of the evidence used in the debate. But looking at the quality leaves out the missing evidence—the studies that could change the debate, or the questions that, in the end, aren't going to be settled by research.

Political scientist Aaron Belkin spent many years studying the military, including the ban on gay people in the U.S. armed forces that was eventually overturned in 2011. Along the way, he developed a useful way to think about research in the context of controversial issues.[7] Once you've got a good list of the issues in the debate, he argues that the key task is sorting them into categories. Some of those arguments will involve appeals to moral or religious values to persuade participants in the debate. Other arguments might be consciously designed to appeal to some emotion that will influence decision makers. Belkin argues that research is not going to be very useful to counter such arguments or influences.

Instead, he focuses on claims of cause and effect or other arguments about consequences. Those arguments make claims like policy X will cause outcome Y. Outcomes could be good or bad, intended or unintended. Either way, the point is that scholars can put those claims to an empirical or logical test. Careful studies of the same policies in other places or contexts might show that those expected consequences do not occur, or manifest to different degrees from what was predicted, for example.

The consequences of high rates of incarceration dominated much of the pre- and post-Ferguson discussion about the criminal justice system. Political scientist Vesla Weaver's research has assessed the social and political consequences for the African American community. In op-eds in the *Baltimore Sun, New York Times*, and *Slate*, she and co-authors argue that mass incarceration destabilizes communities by reducing civic engagement.[8] Her survey data suggest that people in neighborhoods with high incarceration rates begin to see government as something to be avoided. Police stops and arrests reduce people's likelihood of voting, for example, even if they are not convicted. Those who are convicted often cannot vote or serve on juries, adding to their status as second-class citizens. Weaver and her colleagues argue that this sense of disengagement and exclusion leaves protest as the only democratic option left.

The debate about the minimum wage is also all about consequences. The big question is whether a higher minimum wage will cause some workers to lose their jobs, as basic economic theory would suggest. Decades of research have gone into answering that question, and early research seemed to confirm the harmful consequences of the minimum wage. Employers and policymakers used those findings as a brake on many efforts to raise it, so the question about the impact on jobs is also clearly an *important* one in the debate.

Beginning in the 1990s, though, new research methods have suggested that the simple view is misleading. Economist Arin Dube testified on recent research at a U.S. Senate committee hearing in 2013. He reported that a higher minimum wage would actually help employers find and keep employees, balancing out some of the costs of the wage increase. Overall, Dube's reading of his own research and that of other scholars is that the loss of jobs would be very small or maybe even nonexistent, and a higher minimum wage would also have the good consequence of reducing poverty.[9] He has also translated his minimum wage research into op-eds (including a *New York Times* debate) and blog posts.

How do you know if the question you can answer is an important one? Belkin and others from the policy world have argued that the best way to identify and prioritize the questions that emerge from your analysis of a debate is to talk to people in the middle of the debate and decision-making process. Policymakers, attorneys, organizers, and other advocates will have heard the arguments that you've identified and analyzed. They'll have opinions about which ones are the most important to respond to. This is an important role for your network, which we'll get to in chapter 4. Getting the opinions of informed participants in the debate will help you avoid a common academic pitfall: finding a question to focus on that is potentially relevant but is not actually very important.

Translating your own work into the public debate could look very much like the experiences of Dube, Weaver, Ronald, and Belkin. You might have an opportunity to do something similar by taking the first path to connect research and debates and identifying places that research can fit in. Or the second path might lead you to new research on emerging questions in the debate about the impact of a particular policy decision. That kind of analysis takes different forms and might even involve identifying new research projects that you would take on to address the gaps you've identified.

Another Role: Change the Terms of the Debate

Focusing on policy consequences or critical summaries of a debate are not the only ways that scholars can find a role, though. What if you don't like the terms of the debate? You might decide that your contribution is to push the debate in a more productive direction. Game-changing scholars have changed how the public sees the world (see Box 2.5).

If you want to nudge the whole public debate, it's useful to understand why the big picture looks the way it does. How the players in the public debate define the problem to address and the options for solving that problem set the boundaries for the public discussion. The particular options on the table emerge out of a policy and political process that actively shapes the current agenda and framing of a problem. Political horse-trading, interest group jockeying, imperfect information, and ideological disagreement will all be part of the construction of those policy proposals. And those choices are strategic—the problem and options are chosen to steer the eventual decision in a particular direction.[10]

Box 2.5. Four Game-Changing Scholars

Tim Wu, a law professor and one-time computer programmer, is the father of "net neutrality." That principle has influenced advocates and policymakers alike.[a] Net neutrality means requiring broadband providers to treat all Internet content providers equally, not favoring those (such as Netflix) ready to pay more for faster service. Wu and others argue that the Internet should be regulated for the public good like a utility, a goal still being debated.

Law professor **Michelle Alexander's** best-selling book, *The New Jim Crow: Mass Incarceration in the Age of Colorblindness*, shook up our understanding of the American criminal justice system.[b] Alexander's book argues that the war on drugs created a new form of control and subordination of African Americans, starting not long after the civil rights victories in the 1960's. The book documents how mass incarceration of African Americans has far-reaching consequences even for ex-offenders, such as job discrimination, loss of voting rights, and barriers to public benefits. Alexander is a highly visible and persuasive advocate of change, appearing in the news media and at high-profile speaking events before a wide variety of audiences.

Economists **Esther Duflo** and **Abhijit Banerjee** have persuaded many scholars and institutions that the best way to address global poverty is to carefully assess what works in real-world situations. They have pioneered the testing of policy ideas through randomized control trials similar to those used in medical research.[c] By identifying policies and programs that helps poor individuals improve their economic conditions, their work has challenged how global development agencies and economists think about the role of foreign aid to reduce poverty.

a Jeff Somer, "Defending the Open Internet," *New York Times* (May 11, 2014), http://www.nytimes.com/2014/05/11/business/defending-the-open-internet.html.
b Jennifer Schuessler, "Drug Policy as Race Policy: Best Seller Galvanizes the Debate," *New York Times* (March 6, 2012), http://www.nytimes.com/2012/03/07/books/michelle-alexanders-new-jim-crow-raises-drug-law-debates.html.
c Abhijit V. Banerjee and Esther Duflo, *Poor Economics: A Radical Rethinking of the Way to Fight Global Poverty* (New York: PublicAffairs, 2011); Ian Parker, "The Poverty Lab," *New Yorker* (May 17, 2010), 79–89.

You can manage this familiar tension here between lofty goals and political reality, though, especially as your network incorporates some of the people setting those boundaries and as you learn to communicate with a wider variety of audiences. Here are a few possible roles and strategies once you've made that investment.

Shifting the Debate

What is the debate about? You might think that a relatively narrow debate about a particular piece of legislation or proposal misses the larger point. Debates about the Keystone pipeline, offshore oil drilling, or the operation of particular coal-fired power plants might be important in the context of energy policy, for example, but a focus on a specific decision might ignore some broader perspective that your analysis suggests is better, like the need to transition to renewable clean energy sources. Health care reform like the Affordable Care Act might focus on incremental change when widespread systemic change is the only way you see of achieving the twin goals of universal access and affordable coverage. Debates about abstinence-until-marriage sexuality education might miss the point that our culture needs a different approach to understanding adolescent sexuality.

In other words, you might want to shift the debate toward a different view of the issue or problem instead of jumping into the debate about the particular specific issue of the day. Reframing the debate is an important contribution academics can make, although doing so effectively is very difficult, especially with just one individual voice. Once you have a good network, you can work on mobilizing your team to help you.

Expanding the Options

The options for action that are on the table will also certainly shape the debate. If you don't like the options being debated, then your contribution might be offering a new one to consider. Whether your idea will be seen as a serious option will probably depend on its resonance with political actors and on your own ability to be a policy entrepreneur like Teresa Ghilarducci or Daniel Gade, promoting it among people who would need to buy into it.

One tool at your disposal is to look for what political scientists call a "policy window" when your issue becomes a hot topic in the media. As the window opens, new ideas and voices will find it easier to get into the mix. You'll have to pay attention to sense such a shift, and reading the *New York Times* will not be enough. Today social media and the blogosphere might also help create policy windows. Leaks of unexpected information or politicians' scandals, the rapid spread of news about breaking events, and coordinated online advocacy might all help to generate a policy window. Networking with the players in the existing debate, and especially with others who share your goal of shifting the debate, will give you added information and a route to follow once you sense that the timing is right.

For example, recent crises related to public sector pensions and concerns about Social Security's financing opened up a policy window for Ghilarducci. She seized the opportunity to promote her idea of Guaranteed Retirement Accounts for workers. She's found a particularly interested audience in some states.[11] The California Secure Choice Retirement Savings Trust Act will give many more employees an opportunity to save for retirement, with those savings managed by a public agency. Connecticut lawmakers created the Connecticut Retirement Security Board to study and create a proposal for a public retirement plan like the GRA.

Jacob Hacker got labeled as "the father of the public option" in the debate on health care reform. He notes that the title came from "my advocacy for the so-called 'public option,' the idea of creating a Medicare-like public insurance plan to compete with private insurance that became a central issue in the recent health care debates."[12] Although the public option did not become part of the Affordable Care Act, many members of Congress took his option seriously.

Once you're in the middle of a policy process that's likely to result in some kind of action, the need for practical solutions or policy compromises usually means accepting some flaws. Theoretical purity is often an attractive and successful academic strategy, but it doesn't work in politics. Balancing idealism with realism comes with the territory for scholars who want to be effective and influential.

Addressing Emotionally Charged Debates

Some debates involve big issues that seem a long way from facts and ideas. Disputes about gun control or abortion include more visceral arguments that don't lend themselves to a headier cause-and-effect debate, for instance. In situations like these, scholars' contributions might lie in their ability to clarify and understand the emotional or moral basis for those opinions so that other participants in the debate are better informed in their efforts to change or muster the opinions of those individuals.

Scholars can explore answers to many questions about those beliefs: How are they formed? What sustains them in the face of other people's differing opinions? What psychological, political, social, cultural, or economic purposes might those beliefs serve?

What are the important social and psychological characteristics of people who hold those beliefs?

Researchers might even conduct studies that explore ways to change attitudes related to a particular issue. Religious scholars might make arguments about how a different application of particular religious values could lead to an entirely different opinion about an issue like abortion or gay marriage. Or psychologists could apply research that focuses on changing prejudices that people hold.

Creative thinking about ways to use academic research that would take into account the emotional component can be very important.

Using Polling Data

When I've asked politicians or organizations about using research related to their work, their first thoughts usually go to public opinion polls. Polling data influences the media analysis of issues, organizations' political strategies, and politicians' positions. At their best, polls represent a kind of democratic pulse-taking, although obviously one that might be shaped by question wording, ordering, and other important characteristics of surveys. The use of this kind of research offers a great opportunity for scholars' input. Political scientists, psychologists, and sometimes sociologists or economists have provided valuable input into public debates by better measuring and interpreting public opinion on particular issues or elections. Polls are also essential tools for assessing which messages resonate with the public. (And, I would note, they have helped to create new data that could be useful for academic research by other scholars.)

At this point, spend a little time thinking about how to define your role in the debate that you want to be an influential part of.

Box 2.6. Polls to Ponder

Polling is a business. Lots of polling companies are essentially marketing firms that sell their services to businesses, social movements, politicians, and other clients. Much of that work is proprietary and not available to the general public, unless it's through a client or it's about an election. But here are examples of organizations that do regular polling and make some important findings available publicly:

- The Pew Research Center is a well-respected (not-for-profit) source of timely public opinion data: www.pewresearch.org.
- Gallup is a long-time player in the marketing and polling world: www.gallup.com.
- The Field Poll archives its data at the University of California: field.com/fieldpoll/.
- SurveyUSA covers a range of election and other public issues, including what they call "hyper-local" samples: www.surveyusa.com.
- Harris Interactive runs online panels to collect data, including the well-known Harris Poll: www.harrisinteractive.com.
- Fivethirtyeight.com provides comparison and analysis across different polls (and other many other kinds of data). They also rate pollsters based on their historical accuracy in predicting election outcomes.

What are the big questions in the area you want to influence? Which ones are important? Can you offer game-changing contributions to move the debate? Understanding the big picture debate in detail is essential if you want to be proactive and influential. You can also start small, but start smart.

Once you see possible roles for yourself, the next step is to learn more about the people and institutions at the core of the debate. The next chapter takes you down that road to think about "the rules of the game" and the players in the game so you can better plan your role and the best place to begin.

3

Seeing the Big Picture, Part 2
· ·
Mastering the Rules of the Game

After serving as an expert witness in a St. Louis school deseg-regation case, political scientist Gary Orfield was asked by the judge to help school officials and citizens to craft a desegregation plan. They had a daunting task. In 1972, 81% of St. Louis elementary and high schools were highly segregated: 57% were almost all (90% plus) black; 24% were almost all white. Orfield worked out a desegregation plan that moved students via magnet schools and voluntary student transfers between the city and suburbs.[1]

The city had no funding to implement the plan, though, so Orfield tapped into his knowledge of federal court precedents to pry funding out of the state. States were required to act affirmatively to desegregate schools, but research by one of Orfield's colleagues documented admissions by state officials that they had done nothing. As a result, Orfield's report convinced the judge to require the state to finance the new plan, resulting in over a billion dollars in funding.

For Orfield, training in judicial process and experience in the education system enhanced his effectiveness in the courts. For economist Teresa Ghilarducci, implementation details mattered for proposing her policy ideas: "I realized that I couldn't write about pension policy without really understanding how the institutions worked that regulated it."

Orfield and Ghilarducci are masters of the rules of the game. How important are these rules for scholars looking to make a difference in the public realm? Our academic colleagues who study how science is used in public decision-making give us a resounding academic confirmation:

> Focusing on understanding institutional arrangements—how the agencies, departments, and political institutions involved in policy making operate and relate to one another—may be what matters most in improving the connection between science and policy making.[2]

Those rules and arrangements can get pretty complicated, but as you get started it's helpful to keep it simple. In this chapter, we'll take a quick tour of the arenas where the action takes place, looking at the basic rules of the game that answer the who, what, and when of engagement in those arenas:

- *Who decides?* A legislator or judge? Federal, state, or local officials? Or are you trying to influence decisions made by social movement activists, community institutions, business officials, or the general public? The chapter lays out a checklist of sources to identify decision makers and other players in the debate you're interested in.
- *What do they need?* What kinds of research-based information and analysis will decision makers use? The chapter describes the most common uses of research.
- *When and how are research and ideas relevant?* Decision makers might draw on scholars for hearings, briefings, trials, or behind-the-scenes meetings.

Box 3.1. Checklist: Arenas Where Important Decisions Are Made

- Legislatures
- Executive branch agencies, departments, and officials
- Executives: mayors, governors, or president
- Judicial system
- Social movement organizations
- Unions
- Social and health service providers
- Businesses
- Mainstream news media and social media
- Foundations and philanthropists
- Be sure to look across geography:
  - international, national, state, and local governments and nongovernmental organizations
  - multinational, multistate companies

To see the rules in action, let's follow the scholars who study the minimum wage. You don't hear much about efforts to reduce the minimum wage these days, but the debates about raising it are growing louder and more urgent as the gap between rich and poor widens. This chapter walks through a wide range of contexts where this and many other topics are debated. It's worth at least a glance at each stop along the way, even for those arenas that seem less relevant to your own area of interest. Understanding how you fit into these institutions will eventually help you to identify the people you want in your network and to develop your communication strategy. You'll also sound like you know what you're talking about when you start to develop that network. And possibly you'll even get to the point that Orfield and Ghilarducci have reached, where your knowledge of the rules *is* part of your contribution to the public debate. You, too, will be a master of the rules of the game.

Who Decides?

Start with the people who get to decide and look at where they are when they make these decisions. They might be sitting in legislators' offices, in a courtroom, behind a microphone, in a boardroom, on a picket line, or at a bureaucrat's desk. You'll find the minimum wage debated in almost every one of those places these days.

These decision makers will make different kinds of decisions. In the case of the minimum wage, policymakers vote on what the minimum should be, who gets covered, when the change takes place, etc. The general public is deciding which course of action they support, or maybe even they'll be voting directly on whether to raise the minimum in some states. Unions and other social movement groups are deciding how to make noise, while journalists and editors are deciding whether it's news.

Put them on a map: Are these decision makers working at an international, national, state, or local level? The broadest coverage for the minimum wage happens at the federal level, but at this writing twenty-nine states have set it higher, sometimes because voters said yes to ballot initiatives to raise the minimum.[3] Seattle's City Council voted in a $15 an hour minimum, the highest yet in the U.S.

We would see the same geographic distinctions for other issues, too. For instance, a debate about homelessness could take place at all of those levels. International bodies might be monitoring progress toward meeting individuals' human right to housing.[4] The federal government might consider more funding for housing vouchers for low-income people. The state you live in might craft an affordable housing policy or social service programs designed to reduce homelessness. Local communities might consider funding levels or zoning for locations of shelters. One advantage of thinking geographically is that you're likely to have more immediate access to decision makers at the local level, always a good place to start.

In the U.S. context, the branch of government also matters. Is this a judicial, legislative, or executive matter? We mentioned legislators already, but other branches matter, too, for the minimum wage. The executive—the president, governor, or mayor—can direct their staff to prepare policy proposals, and the executive branch is in charge of implementing changes in law. Executives have other cards to play, too: President Obama signed an executive order raising the minimum wage paid by companies that do business with the federal government. Courts enforce laws through the prosecution of accused violators, for example, or by deciding whether laws are constitutional.

Social scientists point to other key actors working in the policy arena. Social movements, unions, private philanthropy (such as foundations), and nonprofit organizations (or nongovernmental institutions—NGOs) are powerful players for social and political change, especially on the minimum wage issue, whether from the political right, left, or center. Even business leaders and their businesses are expected to have some concern for the public interest, either because public policies shape how they operate or because they want to be socially responsible.

Each set of players means different opportunities for engagement in different arenas. Getting onto the playing field will be easier if you're bringing something that somebody needs.

What Do They Need?

Scholars have produced mountains of research on the minimum wage and the people who are affected by it, but not all of it will be directly useful in every part of the policy process. In the last chapter, you saw the tools to understand the big picture and to identify important questions in the debate you want to be a part of, and some of those questions relate directly to research. The players in the debates aren't likely to come to the mountain, so you have to take the useful parts to them.

Here's what they might be on the lookout for:[5]

- *Identifying problems*: Does your work uncover or focus on a new problem? Why is this a problem that should be the subject of a public discussion? (And you might ask whether this problem could resolve itself on its own.) Or do you have a different way of framing a known problem that would take the debate in a different direction? The minimum wage is an old idea with new significance for those concerned about the problem of rising income inequality.[6]
- *Suggesting solutions*: Have you come up with ideas for addressing a particular problem? If your work mostly identifies problems, it's worth thinking about proposing solutions too. You will very likely be asked for possible solutions in the public conversation. The minimum wage is exactly that—a way to reduce inequality by bringing up the incomes of people at the bottom.
- *Evaluating proposed solutions and programs*: Does your work suggest how effective a proposed solution might be at solving or mitigating a problem? Policymakers might see the minimum wage as a way to reduce poverty, but some scholars argue that the minimum wage helps lots of people who aren't poor, so the poverty impact might not be big.

- *Comparing proposed solutions and programs*: This role for research is similar to evaluation, although it's usually called policy analysis. You could compare several policy approaches to reducing income inequality or poverty, such as the Earned Income Tax Credit, higher cash assistance payments, public employment schemes, and the minimum wage. You'd ask the same questions of each policy to see which best achieves your goals: Is it effective in reducing poverty? Is it politically feasible? Is it easy to enforce? Is it allowed by our constitution? Etc.
- *Predicting consequences*: Does your research predict the consequences of adopting a particular policy? That's the does-the-minimum-wage-lead-to-job-loss question again.
- *Assessing whether a situation meets certain specified criteria*: Does your research help decision makers apply some criterion specific to a particular context? You wouldn't ask whether the minimum wage improves air quality, but air quality changes might matter a lot for an environmental issue.

If you have answers to those kinds of questions, you're well on the way to finding a path to engagement in one of these arenas. Of course, you'll also need to communicate those findings in ways that your audience will understand, but more on that in later chapters. If you don't have answers to these or similar questions, you'll need to figure out other ways of getting the attention of decision makers, perhaps through research-related insights into strategies for change.

When and Where Do They Need It?

Legislative Chambers and Backrooms

In general, the legislative process is fairly similar across the different federal, state, and local legislative contexts. A legislator files a piece of legislation to raise the minimum wage, our example, although that bill might be written by a staff member or an issue advocate. The legislation is usually referred to one or more committees where hearings or other information gathering processes occur. The bill might be amended in committee. The committee debates the bill and votes whether to refer it to the main body with a recommendation for passage. The main body has rules (which can vary widely) about how it will take up a bill for consideration and voting. In the end, not all bills are acted on in committee, and even fewer are passed by the main body and sent to the executive for signature.

Legislators and their staffs sometimes talk to researchers informally to get ideas about new legislation that's needed or to improve existing legislation. I met a scholar of the health effects of gambling who sent an email to her state legislator about her research-based concerns about casino legislation. She was pleasantly surprised to get a call within minutes from the legislator, who wanted to know more and eventually incorporated her ideas about funding for research into the legislation.

Because of their focus on consequences, researchers who study the minimum wage often appear as expert witnesses at committee hearings. Economist Heather Boushey testified at a Senate hearing that a higher minimum wage would pull more than 6 million people out of poverty.[7] The previous year, policy analyst James Sherk had argued before the same committee that there would be little effect on poverty.[8]

Testimony is the most formal and visible role for researchers in the legislative context, but you don't typically see the intense and detailed cross-examination of the courtroom. Legislators are usually the only ones allowed to ask questions—a sight that would be familiar to watchers of C-SPAN, which is an excellent place to see this process in action. While the questions and answers might sound academic, it's more about politics and making a point than education.

Politics also play a big role in who gets invited to testify. In Congress, the rules of the game favor the majority party, which gets more time in the hearing to present its point of view by inviting most of the witnesses. In state legislatures or local legislative bodies, though, testimony time is usually much more open to the public and is often up for grabs in a first-come, first-served system.

In committee hearings, bill sponsors and advocates often want to invite experts whose testimony supports the framing of the problem and the fix addressed by the legislation. Other experts might appear at the request of opponents of the bill. As Chris Hellman, a think tank veteran, once explained at a workshop, the education has already happened by the time the hearing rolls around, and the experts are often there simply *to validate* a point that the members already believe.[9] Some experts (particularly legal scholars) play a more technical role, identifying concerns and possible fixes in the public hearing, often points that have been made in informal contexts.

But studies of the way research is used in legislative contexts suggest that our knowledge isn't just used to back up policymakers' prior opinions. Karen Bogenschneider and Thomas Corbett interviewed policymakers who reported changing their opinions after learning of research findings, particularly when research dispels myths or where values and ideology were not so important.[10] Timely, accessible, and credible research can help politicians gain the respect of their colleagues and constituents and build support for legislation.[11]

The Courtroom

Courts come into play in the interpretation and enforcement of laws. Academics are asked to give—and defend—their expert opinions on many subjects in court.

Most of the time those expert opinions address the application of specific laws, so understanding the statutes and regulations in a particular area would be important. Some businesses quickly sued Seattle over its $15 an hour minimum wage, although it's too soon to tell whether the case will involve experts from academia. It's easy to find examples of social scientists involved in cases, though. In 1999, MIT economists Richard Schmalensee and Franklin Fisher testified on opposite sides in a big antitrust lawsuit against Microsoft, disagreeing on the degree of competition and monopoly power in the computer industry. Sociologist William Bielby testified in a high-profile sex discrimination lawsuit against Wal-Mart, arguing that the company's personnel policies made decisions about wages and promotion of women "vulnerable to gender bias."[12]

Less frequently, but more visibly, experts might be called into cases where constitutional rights are at stake. Laws passed by legislatures or by referendum must be consistent with state and federal constitutions, or else courts can strike down those laws. When a case goes to court, lawyers on both sides turn to scholars for research they can use as evidence to bolster their arguments. Scholars may end up debating the interpretation of data, critiquing each other, and predicting the future to give judges a basis for making a decision.

For instance, a 2003 Supreme Court case on the constitutionality of the campaign finance law known as McCain-Feingold pit-

Box 3.2. The View from the Expert Witness Box

I've had one experience in that box myself in 2010. I'd been hired by the attorneys for the City and County of San Francisco and for Kris Perry, Sandy Stier, Jeff Zarrillo, and Paul Katami. The two same-sex couples sat thirty feet in front of me, reminding me of what was at stake. They had sued the State of California for violating the U.S. Constitution by taking away their right to marry after the statewide referendum known as Proposition 8 passed in 2008. Directly in front of me (most of the time) was an attorney from the other side—defending Proposition 8—who grilled me on the details of my opinions, including my research that showed that losing the right to marry would be economically harmful for same-sex couples and for the state's budget. There was one big difference between that give and take and the usual academic wrangling over research findings: On my right sat Judge Vaughan Walker, who was the referee. He would decide whether my testimony— and that of the many other scholars testifying on both sides in the case—was understandable, credible, and relevant to his decision. Ultimately, Judge Walker agreed that same-sex couples and their families were harmed and that the state had no rational basis for denying same-sex couples the right to marry.[a]

---

a Marriages of same-sex couples resumed in 2013 only after the U.S. Supreme Court ruled in *Hollingsworth v. Perry*, as the case was known then, that the organization that had intervened to defend Proposition 8 had no legal standing to do so.

ted political scientists against each other (*McConnell v. FEC*). Ray LaRaja and Sidney Milkis took the side of the plaintiffs filing the suit, and Jonathan Krasno and Frank Sorauf testified for the federal government, which was defending the suit. Even in the adversarial context of a high-profile court case, those four agreed that the case gave them an opportunity to apply their academic work and to engage in an important debate through the case without violating their integrity as social scientists.[13]

Executive Branch Bureaucracies

The executive branch of government implements laws. Generally, specific agencies take statutes and create rules and regulations to provide detailed instructions about how a law like the minimum wage law will work. At the federal level, scholars have at least a few options for influencing the executive branch. When agencies add or change rules or regulations, they must give the public a chance to comment on the changes.[14] Also, agencies usually have to show that the benefits of a rule change outweigh any costs, and they sometimes look to academic research to come up with estimates of those costs and benefits. Also, some federal agencies have advisory boards that provide opportunities for knowledgeable outsiders or constituents to give feedback and advice. Getting onto one of those boards is not easy, and that's where a broad network can help. Public meetings are another, less regular opportunity to weigh in. A less common route to influence is getting a political appointment by an executive (the president or governor) to take on a role within an agency (see Box 3.3).

Private Sector: Businesses

Many laws limit businesses' ability to take actions that are not in the public interest. They can't discriminate against women in employment, they must abide by contract law, their right to pollute is constrained, etc. However, businesses sometimes voluntarily change their practices even without being required to do so. For example, clothing retailer The Gap, Inc., voluntarily boosted the lowest wage it pays to $9 in 2014 and $10 in 2015.[15] So debates over big issues play out in private as well as public arenas, making the private sector a possible arena for action.

Box 3.3. Scholars Who Became Policymakers

- **Samantha Power**, who taught at Harvard's Kennedy School of Government, served in President Obama's National Security Council and later as the United States ambassador to the U.N.

- **Cass Sunstein** moved from his position as professor of law and political science at the University of Chicago to lead the White House Office of Information and Regulatory Affairs from 2009 to 2012.

- Health economist **Sherry Glied** (now dean of NYU's Wagner Graduate School of Public Service) shuttled between Columbia University and Washington, D.C., serving on President Bill Clinton's Council of Economic Advisors in 1992–93 and as assistant secretary for planning and evaluation at the Department of Health and Human Services in the Obama administration in 2010–12.

- Senator **Elizabeth Warren** was elected from Massachusetts while a Harvard law professor.

- Former secretary of state **Condoleeza Rice** returned to her roots as a political science professor at Stanford University after working in President George W. Bush's administration.

- Representative **Dina Titus** was elected to Congress from Nevada, where she was a professor of political science at the University of Nevada, Las Vegas, until 2011.

Large companies whose stocks are traded publicly are responsible to their shareholders, who are the actual owners of the corporation and can demand a vote on certain changes in policy. Socially responsible investment advocates often try to use that process to change corporate policies.[16]

Businesses also reconsider and adapt their internal policies through internal processes that involve some kind of chain of command up to the decision maker, often the CEO. Outsiders, usually working with insiders, have an opportunity to influence those decisions.

The most effective argument for a business is an appeal to the bottom line—profit. Scholars (myself included) are often involved in helping employees and other stakeholders use research to make the "business case" for higher wages, family-friendly policies, domestic partner benefits, or environmental responsibility, for example. Businesses pay attention if you can show that their revenues will go up or their costs will go down—either way, their profits rise. Higher profits make managers and stockholders very happy and much more likely to make the change advocated. Businesses will sometimes adopt policies that raise their costs, but it helps if research shows that cost increase is quite small, as it has been when employers offer health care benefits to employees' unmarried domestic partners, for example.

Businesses also participate in public debates, both as donors to candidates or political organizations, and more publicly as direct advocates of policies that they see as central to their business success. But they might also be responsive to pushback from shareholders, customers, and employees.

Private Sector: Foundations

Foundations are players in many parts of the social change game. They usually do not fund advocacy or research that's designed only for lobbying. But foundations do provide resources that support social services, community organizations, research, and educational efforts, depending on their mission. Getting a grant from an influential foundation like Ford, Rockefeller, or Gates also legitimates the work that's funded, and it enhances the status of grantees. Even if a foundation does not fund research per se, it might sometimes commission research or consult with scholars in a particular field to understand pressing needs and effective organizations in the context that foundation works in, for example.

In this case, understanding the rules of the game involves good "grantspersonship"—understanding the foundation's mission, funding guidelines, and decision-making process. Look carefully at past and current grantees to get a sense of what the foundation is trying to do. You need to find a hook to convince the foundation's staff that you have something useful to offer, either as a grantee or consultant on broader policy issues.

Influential development economist Esther Duflo has effectively leveraged connections with donors like Bill Gates, who supports her work, and an alumnus who endowed the research center she co-founded, the Abdul Latif Jameel Poverty Action Lab at MIT.[17] Foundation and donor partnerships don't always produce support at that scale, of course, but it's useful to dream big.

Social Movements: Activists and Organizations

Social movements—activists and their advocacy organizations—are central to the process of social change for many issues. Organizations like the National Employment Law Project, Let Justice Roll, Fast Food Forward, and the National Women's Law Center, as well as unions like the Service Employees International Union (SEIU) and the AFL-CIO, have funded and led the political movement to increase the minimum wage, including strikes against fast food restaurants across America.

If you want to influence what's on the agenda or how it's framed, whether you identify as an activist-scholar or not, you might want to work with or through these organizations in some way. Movements are a primary source of the policy agenda.

Box 3.4. Ideas for Finding Funding for Public-Oriented Research[a]

- Read acknowledgements of articles and reports for names of funders that support research for scholars doing work in the area you want to engage in.
- Frame your plan for public engagement as involving the kind of "broader impact" that the National Institutes of Health and the National Science Foundation require.
- Look for funders of "translational" research taking academic work into real-world settings.
- Partner with community organizations or other nonprofits on grant applications. Those collaborations show foundations that you are committed to making your research relevant and accessible to people who know how to work for social change.
- Some foundations are known to be particularly interested in social change or social justice efforts, and some of these want their research funding to make an impact:
  - Ford Foundation (a wide range of social and economic issues): www.fordfoundation.org
  - Bill & Melinda Gates Foundation (health, development, and education): www.gatesfoundation.org
  - William T. Grant Foundation (youth issues): wtgrantfoundation.org
  - Carnegie Corporation of New York (education, peace, and security): www.carnegie.org
  - Spencer Foundation (education): www.spencer.org

Box 3.4. Ideas for Finding Funding for Public-Oriented Research (*cont.*)

- Annie E. Casey Foundation (issues related to children): www. aecf.org
- Open Society Foundations (range of issues including human rights, democracy, education, and health): www. opensocietyfoundations.org
- MacArthur Foundation (range of issues including human rights, reproductive health, education, and economic development): www.macfound.org
- If you want to locate potential sources of funding for research, try these tools:
- Access searchable databases, such as the Foundation Directory Online (from the Foundation Center) or Foundation Search (a for-profit site).
- Read sections of publications about academia, such as the new grants published in *The Chronicle of Higher Education*. More specialized publications include *The Chronicle of Philanthropy* and *Inside Philanthropy* (www.insidephilanthropy.com).
- The Foundation Center offers various online resources, including http://www.grantcraft.org, http://www.grantspace. org, and http://www.foundationcenter.org.
- Your university might have an office to help scholars find private foundation support for their research.

a Thanks to Susan Newton at UMass Amherst for many of these ideas.

Organizations produce public education, litigation, publications, advertisements, community gatherings, and lobbying, and each of those activities might benefit from some kind of research or new ideas. As I'll discuss in a later chapter, these organizations can play an important role for engaged scholars, acting as leverage or knowledge accelerators for academics. If your knowledge is useful to them, they will carry it forward into policymaking or other contexts for you!

In working with social movements, the rules of the game are not easy to characterize. Organizations and coalitions have goals that involve a mission, usually involving political and social change—civil rights, environmental regulation, financial system reform, or health care access, for example. To achieve those goals, they want to pass legislation or convince other decision makers to make some kind of institutional change. Unions have a more direct goal of improving the wages and working conditions of their members or future members through collective bargaining and changes in public policy.

Decision making within movement organizations is complex. Organizations that are incorporated and have a tax-exempt status might have some constraints on their political activities. Membership organizations (particularly unions) might provide a grassroots means to influence policy within an organization, but not all social movement organizations are structured that way. In other organizations, staff members and management will likely have a decision-making process, and a board of directors has policy-making authority and sets strategy. Also, large donors' opinions will sometimes have influence over board and staff decisions.

And there's another issue to consider: The nature of movement goals means that organizational priorities might not always be compatible with our goals as researchers. Sociologist Sara

Goldrick-Rab, who studies how to make college more affordable, identifies as a "scholar-activist," not an advocate. The distinction matters to her. "An advocate begins with a core and guiding goal—not a theory—and pushes for changes to achieve that goal," she writes. "In contrast, a scholar-activist begins with a set of testable assumptions, subjects these to rigorous research, and once in possession of research findings seeks to translate those findings into action."[18] Social movement organizations usually have their own understanding about how the world works, and they are not always interested in testing that understanding. In fact, research that might undermine that understanding could be very threatening.

Other challenges of working with social movements include managing diverse strategies and viewpoints across organizations involved in a single movement. Investing a little time in learning about the history of a movement you want to work within can help you understand why there are so many different organizations and what their stated and actual roles are within the movement. That history leads to expectations and access to resources for particular organizations that become part of the rules of the game.

Despite those challenges, the rewards of working with social movements can be enormous. Those movements can provide a second home for scholars whose own values are aligned with movement goals, as well as provide a context for deep engagement with the process of change that has motivated many of us, myself included, to become scholars in the first place.

Think Tanks

One type of organization, the think tank or public research organization, has played a particularly important and clear role for academics involved in the policy process, including those working with many social movements. The conservative movement in the United States has been extremely effective in mobilizing scholars into think tanks that interact directly with policymakers and advocacy organizations.[19] Now most highly visible political issues have at least one think tank dedicated to research and analysis on that issue, often located in Washington, D.C. Several have been influential in producing and promoting research related to the minimum wage debates: The Economic Policy Institute supports an increase, while the Employment Policies Institute does not, for example.

I use the term "think tank" broadly to define a place that coordinates research on a particular topic for a variety of potential audiences. The work produced by those research organizations ranges widely from misleading propaganda to actual scientific research, so it's important to read a think tank's products carefully to understand in advance where a particular organization fits into that spectrum.

Think tanks can show up in universities, too, staking out a more scholarly end of the spectrum. Gary Orfield's Civil Rights Project, for example, has called Harvard and UCLA home. The Council on Contemporary Families, co-founded by Stephanie Coontz, is a kind of virtual think tank involving scholars from many universities. Sara Goldrick-Rab founded Wisconsin HOPE (Harvesting Opportunities for Postsecondary Education) Lab to use research to increase access to college for low-income students, students of color, and first-generation college students. I worked with others to build the Williams Institute on Sexual Orientation and Gender Identity Law and Public Policy, located at UCLA, which conducts social science and legal research that is relevant to policy and social debates about lesbian, gay, bisexual, and transgender people.

In my view, the think tanks that produce social value act as bridges between the rigorous introspection of academia and the more rough-and-tumble world of politics.[20] Think tanks can pull researchers and policymakers together on relatively neutral territory. Influential think tanks use a variety of communication genres and methods to inject scholarship into policy debates. Perhaps most importantly, think tanks prioritize work on questions that are directly relevant to a public debate rather than the theory-driven questions favored by university scholars.

Working with think tanks feels more like home to many academics. Think tank researchers often have Ph.D.s and are usually fluent in the theoretical and methodological languages of academia. At a superficial level, the rules of the game even seem a lot like those of a research grant. You might be hired to write a paper on a subject you know about, or to conduct a new research project that fits into your disciplinary field and the think tank's sphere of influence.

Other features are quite different, though. Think tanks are considered successful to the degree that their work is visible and influential in policy debates. As a result, the timeline for your project will probably be short to meet some need in the debate. You'll be expected to write something that's accessible and relevant to a nonacademic audience, and you might be expected to participate in public discussions or private briefings of policymakers. And if your findings don't fit the think tank's perspective, your report might never see the light of day. In other words, it might look like academia, but you're much closer to the heart of the policy process when you work with most think tanks.

Conclusion

As this quick tour suggests, there are many different arenas and types of players in big public debates, some obvious (like legislators) and some that might not be so obvious (like businesses). Use these locations as a checklist to get you started, but be prepared to expand it when you're more familiar with your debate. Even a relatively simple issue like the minimum wage debate involves many points of decision making and many players that might seem to take surprising positions, like the pro–minimum wage businesses, until you know more about why they do what they do. Understanding a few specific rules for the major potential players should help you sharpen your big picture, locate the important players, and identify where you might step in. Once you're in the game, you'll learn more about the specific rules that will apply to your particular issue.

In addition to describing the contexts that you might work in, this chapter has also outlined the first step to strategically and consciously building a network. The second step flows directly from this tour of key arenas. Once you have a fuller idea of the big picture—what the arguments are, where the debate is taking place, who the players are, and the basic rules of the game—you're ready to start building that network.

4

Effective Networking
· · · · · · · · · · · · · ·

In 1987, psychiatrist Judith Lipton attended a conference in Moscow on nuclear weapons and disarmament, a field she had been active in for years. She took a copy of the book she co-authored with psychologist David Barash on the nuclear arms race, *The Caveman and the Bomb*, to a party that Mikhail Gorbachev was scheduled to attend.[1]

Although she never got the chance to meet the Soviet leader, Lipton did meet someone who was going to have dinner with Gorbachev the next night. That new acquaintance agreed to pass along the book—and she apparently followed through on her promise. Two years later, the authors found out through a friend of a friend, who had gotten this news from a well-placed professional contact, that their book was translated for Gorbachev and greatly influenced his views about disarmament.

Even though the book by Barash and Lipton sold fewer than a thousand copies, networking got their book into one powerful person's hands. And it took a network to let Barash and Lipton know that they had influenced his thinking.

Finding yourself only a few degrees of separation from the most powerful people in the world isn't implausible. For example, President Obama used to be a professor, so chances are pretty good that you know someone who knows someone who used to work with him at the University of Chicago Law School. To be effective in promoting change with your work, you need to get your ideas and research into the hands of the people who can change things, most of whom won't be at the levels of Obama or Gorbachev. Networks are how that will happen.

Most scholars know how to network, even if we don't think of it that way. We speak in person and communicate with each other through our journal articles, on conference panels, in on-campus seminars, and in blogs. We know how to find each other. Contacting someone whose research is related to your own is mostly as simple as googling a name or going to a university website to track down an email address. We know how to stay well connected to the people we want to reach.

As professionally important as that kind of networking is, it will not get you very far if you want to influence public discussions, policy debates, and actual outcomes. The debate you need to be a part of takes place outside of academia. If you interact with people who aren't academics, you might already have some good links. Political scientist Richard Engstrom became an expert witness in a court case after he happened to meet an attorney at a party.[2] Robert E. Crew, Jr., began applying his political science knowledge as a campaign consultant by tapping into the network of contacts he had built as a volunteer on many local campaigns.[3] Congressman John Boehner was connected to Notre Dame University, where Teresa Ghilarducci once taught, so he would welcome her as a minority witness at congressional hearings.

The problem is that when it comes to finding people on the outside who should know about our work, most academics quickly run out of relevant contacts. Cultivating a network of contacts that includes the people and places you want to influence is one of the essential practices of a scholar who wants to have a practical impact or public presence.

Networks work in both directions. You have something useful to offer the people you want to meet and influence. The people in your network also have something useful to offer you in terms of feedback about your ideas or new information. To the extent that the people you network with understand your ideas and research and recognize its value, they will take your ideas into many more settings than you would ever have access to. In one very real sense, a measure of your influence will be the size of your network.

This chapter presents several different tools, including a way to assess your current network and strategies for building or growing your network. Identifying the playing field was actually the first step in this building process. Here we'll take the places that the debate occurs as starting points for imagining what you want your network to look like. We'll add in your existing network and then figure out how to connect your actual network with the one that will make you influential.

A network is kind of like your team on the playing field of a debate, but thinking about it like a garden might be a more helpful approach. Growing a network means planting lots of seeds, doing some thinning, replanting if the first seeds don't take, replacing plants that don't produce, nurturing your plants from seedlings to mature plants, and harvesting. Gardening also involves the recognition that not every condition will be exactly right and that success involves some luck. Flexibility, perseverance, and learning are all signs of a good gardener who is likely to have a thriving garden. We will draw on those same virtues to grow a network.

Growing Your Network—Planning Out Your Garden

Over the long winters where I live, gardeners start dreaming about what they want to grow, often poring over seed catalogs and ordering seeds to match up their gardens to their imagined pleasure at the harvest many months later. Your networking equivalent might be thinking about how you envision your engagement. Are you talking into a microphone on a radio show? Fielding reactions to an op-ed you wrote in a newspaper? Responding to comments on one of your blog posts? Meeting with legislators at the state capitol? Speaking in front of a group of local activists? Getting your work cited in legislative reports, court decisions, or interest group messages? Even if you aren't sure where exactly you *will* end up, a little imagination about where you *might* want to be can help.

Also, seeds don't just grow on their own. They get planted in a particular plot, and careful gardeners match plots with the sun, soil, and water needs of their plants. In the networking context, you're looking for the places that will provide the resources that your seeds of influence and connection need. The kind of contexts that the debate takes place in should determine where you'll plant your seeds. You want to choose a place that has the nutrients your network will need. Later in this chapter, I'll talk a little about those resources, including time, assistance, and communication methods.

Let's start with the people in the contexts that you want to influence. Box 4.1 is a short checklist of places drawn mostly from other chapters to sketch out where debates take place and decisions get made. Once you've identified the relevant general contexts, this chapter will help you start building out from them to specific individuals, eventually connecting you to those contexts.

Suppose you're interested in policies to promote green and sustainable energy sources or policies to make educational outcomes

Box 4.1. Checklist of Places to Network

1. Courts
2. Legislatures (and other legislative bodies, such as school boards)
3. Executive branch agencies
4. Professional organizations (policies and practices)
5. Foundations
6. Businesses
7. Unions
8. Political parties
9. Social movement organizations
10. Community organizations
11. Think tanks
12. Relevant media outlets
13. Social media contacts

more equitable across race, class, and gender groups. Your analysis of the debates and rules of the game suggest that your issue will mostly be dealt with through the political process (as opposed to, for instance, the judicial system and courts), with legislative bodies on the frontline of the institutional contexts that you want to influence. Now you know where to plant your network seeds.

The next stage is to stake out some boundaries and see what you've got to work with. In the legislative context, the options are finite: Congress, state legislatures, city councils (or county equivalents), school boards, town meetings, and perhaps other elected bodies that make law and set policy. Those bodies might have commissions, committees, and subcommittees. Chances are good that all of these bodies could be relevant in either an environmental or educational context. Most educational policies are set at the local or state level. Environmental policy is more commonly set at the federal or state level, but local governments have become more active in encouraging renewable energy.

You'll probably also want to think about the executive branch. The president and governors have a lot of influence in these areas. They—and their cabinet-level departments and agencies—develop proposals for new policies and carry out past policy decisions. Mayors, commissioners, committee chairs, and other leaders of those bodies might also fit into this category.

Of course, many other individuals and groups will have opinions about and be working on these policy issues, although not all will be organized and easily identifiable. The obvious interest groups in the energy example would be utilities that produce energy and businesses that are big consumers of energy or producers of fossil fuels. A large environmental social movement exists, as well. In the education realm, the big nongovernmental players are teachers and their unions, parents and their organizations, and in some cases, organized groups of students. Administrators have their own professional organizations, and when education policy is debated in Washington, state governments and their organizations also get involved.

Some of those players are advocates, but don't turn away from the more obviously political groups in the name of "staying above the fray." Legislators often get a lot of information about an issue from advocacy-oriented groups or even constituents.[4] (Universities per se are usually much farther down the list of go-to sources, by the way.) Getting your research in the hands of those groups might get it to a decision maker more quickly than your own individual efforts to connect.

I find it helpful to map out the players. Box 4.2 has a simple, rather generic map of an environmental policy issue that captures something that already looks like a network. I put researchers in

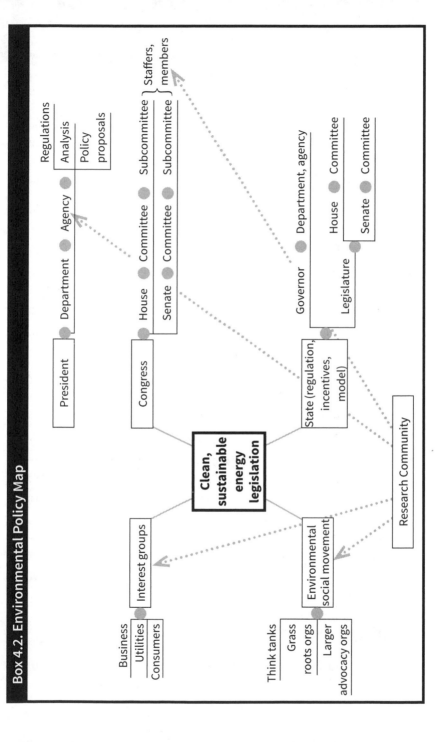

Box 4.2. Environmental Policy Map

the map (and you will want connections to other researchers in your area), with a few lines to show some common connections between the rest of these players and us.

Let me first point out one essential but possibly surprising feature of this networking exercise: Researchers are not at the center! I'll make this more specific: *You* are not at the center of a policy network. I'm assuming that your goal is to use your knowledge and ideas to make some kind of change in the world, so I've put that change at the center of the network diagram.

While engagement can have many positive professional effects, putting your professional self at the conceptual center can be counterproductive when you're building a strong network. You will need to convince influential people and organizations that you can be of help or service to them. They will not work with you because you need them in order to get a grant, promotion, or book contract. They will work with you because you have something that *they* need, so ask them how you can be useful. If you are perceived as too high-maintenance, organizations will figure that out and might avoid working with you. You are the gardener who must tend to your budding contacts and build relationships and trust over time—but unlike in the garden metaphor, you and your contacts reap the harvest.

Box 4.3 gives you a slightly different direction to work from if this more abstract method doesn't work. You can reverse engineer a network if you have a good example to work from. Study a policy proposal that you like to see how it developed and who developed it.

Planting Seeds

Now that you've identified the places you want access to, you've got some idea about where you want to plant. Next, you need to

---

Box 4.3. Another Path: Reverse Engineering a Network

Here's another way to get started with identifying contexts and players. Pick an existing proposal to deal with a problem you're interested in. Interpret the term "proposal" broadly. You might have heard of an actual piece of legislation, maybe because of a controversy, hearing, or vote on the bill. Or you might have heard an idea discussed in the media or at a conference. Either way, track it down.

Identify the players or stakeholders:

• Who suggested this proposal or idea? Or who wrote the bill?
• Which organizations are working to get it passed?
• Which elected officials have endorsed it or, if it's a bill, who sponsored it? Who's the lead sponsor?
• Who opposes it?
• Who favors it?
• Where does the information cited in advocates' talking points or publications come from?
• Who is reporting on this issue in the media? Which advocates and experts do they interview?

Then map those players out!

---

prepare the ground just a bit more to find the specific people you want to meet and work with. Remember that even those faceless institutional categories are made up of organizations of some kind—like specific corporations, NGOs, or legislative offices—that are run by people. You need to put some names of real people and organizations next to those labels.

This step requires a little digging. You'll find plenty of information about organizations and companies on official websites. Look at the history of relevant institutions and organizations to get a sense of which ones best fit your own take on an issue. Get a sense of how they do their work: Are they businesses or nonprofits? Do they have members? Who's on their boards? What kind of work do they do—lobbying, education, research, services, manufacturing? Where do they do this work? What are they trying to change or accomplish?

Finding an organization chart helps to understand better where the organizations' resources go. An online staff directory or organization chart will often give you the names of people who work there—the jackpot, especially if the chart comes with emails and phone numbers.[5]

Usually the hardest part is deciding exactly who you're looking for. You want someone who is in a position to understand your work and how it might relate to their own needs. Here are a few general suggestions to think about:

- *Businesses*: Communications, public relations, or government relations people might seem to be a logical choice, but they aren't necessarily a good place to start. While people in those positions are externally oriented, they are not the people you're likely to be working with on a specific substantive issue, so I would encourage you to skip over those offices and go more directly to your ultimate goal. For example, if you're interested in workplace policy, look for human resources officials or a diversity manager, or find relevant employee resource groups or union officials. If you're concerned about environmental issues, look for an office that works on compliance on those issues. Trade associations and groups for business professionals, such as the Society for Human Resource Management, might present opportunities to find potential contacts who are connected to relevant people in many companies.
- *Nonprofits*: Look for the offices or titles that seem to be most closely related to what you're interested in. Titles like "policy director" might seem like obvious people to talk to. However, often those are the folks

doing lobbying, and they might not be what you're after. Many large organizations now have some kind of research department, even if that's not their main activity. Although the researchers might not be people in your field (or even people with Ph.D.s), they are often the best place to start to tie into an organization. Read a few reports of interest to you and note the names of authors.

- *Elected officials*: The vast majority of elected officials are people you can talk to directly without deep layers of staff standing in your way. Some will have a secretary and perhaps only an assistant or two unless they chair a committee or have some larger role. The higher up you go, the more likely you are to need to look for staffers to talk to. At the congressional level, committees also have their own staffs, and many of those people will know a lot about the issues their committee deals with. The staffs of individual members will usually be generalists, although a powerful member's large staff might also include people with particular interests and areas of expertise. Get to know these policymakers—research suggests that "policymakers respond to people they know and trust" when it comes to research.[6]

- *Government agencies*: Many of the suggestions from above apply here. Most of the basic structure of state and federal government agencies can be gleaned from websites. Agencies are sometimes more protective of employee names and organizational structures, though, so you might need to dig harder to figure out who you want to reach out to. Large agencies that must report outcomes to federal funders or to a data-driven governor are likely to have at least a small research or statistical staff. Look at the names of people on reports or press releases from those offices.

- *Media*: Understanding media coverage of an issue can help your networking efforts in at least two ways. First, you might want to cultivate some ties with journalists or bloggers who write about the issues at the level you want to engage—local, state, national, or international.

This part is relatively easy. Finding out who has your issue's beat at newspapers is usually as simple as seeing who writes the articles that catch your eye. Second, the news that gets reported might include interviews and quotes from people in the institutions you want to reach, providing an invaluable source of names of actual people to seek out. Likewise, key people in other social media, particularly Twitter, are helpful to identify early on.

Once you know the names or at least the titles of the people you want to meet, I recommend a combination of direct and indirect approaches. When you've got a few contacts, you can ask those people to recommend others to talk to.

Making Contact and Cultivating Your Contacts

Making Warm Calls

Making contact with the people you've identified is not an exact science. Sometimes the only approach is what salespeople call a "cold call"—you call or write to someone who does not know you and might have absolutely no interest in what you have to offer.

Cold calls can work, especially if you have already developed a reputation and expertise. Through chutzpah and faith in a good idea, environmental chemist Jennifer Field cold-called drug policy specialists until she found one who could help her apply a new technique for monitoring crystal meth use by testing cities' waste water.[7] Twice Teresa Ghilarducci wrote congratulatory notes to new leaders (Indiana governor Frank O'Bannon and President Bill Clinton) and offered them some ideas about pension reform as well as her help. Those letters got passed down through inter-

Box 4.4. Creating and Mobilizing a Network to Address Students' Food Insecurity

Sociologist Sara Goldrick-Rab's research team at her Wisconsin HOPE Lab found evidence that college students from low-income families struggled to afford food. Drawing on those research findings, she mobilized a network to learn about and take action on the issue. The lab organized a workshop on students' food insecurity, bringing together policymakers and practitioners from different campuses. To figure out why it's so hard to meet students' food needs on campus, Goldrick-Rab connected with a workshop participant from the College and Universities Food Bank Alliance, and also drew on her past ties with another nonprofit, Single Stop USA. She expanded her network to include student groups and individual students as they work to create a food pantry on her own campus.[a]

a Sara Goldrick-Rab, "On Scholarly Activism," *Contexts* (blog) (December 4, 2014), http://contexts.org/blog/on-scholarly-activism/.

nal networks, and both times she was asked to be on important boards as a result.

However, if you've done your homework, most of the people you'll be contacting will actually involve warmer calls. Given *their* work and responsibilities, the people you're trying to reach are likely to be interested in *your* work. Ideally, you'll also have a name of a mutual acquaintance to drop, or better yet, an introduction by your mutual friend.

An email message to introduce yourself and a pledge to follow up soon with a phone call can be one good way to test the waters. You might get an enthusiastic response to your email that encourages you to call, or a suggestion of another person who is better suited to talk to you. Even if you get no response to your email, you might have someone who just took you literally and will pick up the phone for a chat once you do call.

Use Your Network for Introductions

My preferred initial communication method, though, and one that I'm always happy to help people with, is the introduction via a common connection.

- If you know someone who knows the person you want to talk to, ask your mutual acquaintance or friend to introduce you, in person or via email.
- If you use LinkedIn, Facebook, or some other social networking site, see if you have a mutual connection (preferably a real one), and use it. If you don't yet use those tools, you should just for this professional networking value alone.[8]
- Look at the advisory boards or alumni lists of your department, college, or university to see if you have an institutional connection to someone who might know your targeted contact.

In other words, tap into your existing networks to build the new network you want to develop. See Box 4.4 for an example.

Don't overlook your academic network. In fact, it's important to develop relationships with other scholars who work on the issues that you also care about, as Gary Orfield, the political scientist who works on civil rights and school desegregation, points out: "the most important contacts I have made have been with networks of researchers from many disciplines and activists and policymakers working on social policy."[9] You'll never know everything about an issue, so having colleagues from other disciplines to draw on will both expand your knowledge and connect you to their networks.

Stephanie Coontz actively cultivates networks of researchers and advises us to be generous. She closely follows and cites other researchers' work on families in her own op-eds. She also makes a point of sending journalists to the specialists in an area. Why does she spend so much time on these efforts? "First of all, you're doing something good," she says. "You're expanding the work of other people whose work is good. But you're also creating that kind of network where they're more likely, then, to send someone to *you* when your expertise is what could be used."[10]

Creating or expanding a network of scholars related to your public interests is a powerful strategy. In addition to its professional and networking value, building a larger professional network on an issue leverages your own time and energy into even more opportunities for contributing to social change. Professional networks can help push our professional organizations to be more publicly relevant, educating the public and helping to shape a public dialog. Working within our professions can also help expand the voices heard, for instance giving scholars of color and women more opportunities to be engaged in important public debates.

Find a Hook

When you make that first communication effort with someone you want to know, you can also mention some recent policy event or organizational accomplishment as a hook. Referring to something recent (such as a new report, the introduction or the signing of a bill, or the hiring of a new executive director) will establish your knowledge about the debate and provide a little practical gloss to enhance your academic credibility and usefulness.

For instance, when you read a journalist's report on a topic you know something about or about an interesting person, you can send the journalist or the interesting person a summary or link to a study you've done that explores a dimension they hadn't thought about.[11] Political scientist Melissa Michelson read a local newspaper article about some innovative ideas for registering Latino voters offered by Warren Slocum, a county registrar of voters in California. She called him up to talk about evaluating his efforts and started a professional relationship that led to a white paper and academic studies of get-out-the-vote experiments.[12]

Later on, events become opportunities to reconnect and nurture your network contacts. After you've established a connection with someone, a new publication, some new testimony you've given, or some other relevant event on your end can also be an opportunity to reconnect.

Build In Some Face Time

The best way to make contact, though, is in person. Academics can develop and carry on relationships with colleagues for years through email without laying eyes on each other. But in the political world, where people spend more time in meetings and much less time than we do behind a computer, face time matters. To become a go-to resource on part of a debate, you need to be a vivid presence in the minds and memories of the other participants. Plus there is no substitute for a real conversation in a social setting to hear the scuttlebutt about an issue, its progress, and key players. People in the policy world will tell you much more in person than they would ever put in an email.

It's much easier than you might think to meet the people you want to know in person.

- *Get to know your state and local elected officials.* They are literally our neighbors and community members. Find out what they look like and start cultivating relationships when you run into them around town. I once ran into the governor of the state I lived in while we were waiting for prescriptions to be filled at a local pharmacy.
- *Volunteer at an organization you want to cultivate ties with.* Social movement organizations and other nonprofit groups often rely on volunteers to do basic office work. Even stuffing envelopes can give you a chance to learn about an organization and to meet some of the staff. When you see opportunities to connect your research with the group's work, you'll already know the people to talk to.
- *Go to events and fundraisers related to your issue or the people and groups involved in your issue.* Most organizations have fundraisers for a variety of giving levels. If your budget does not allow you to attend a lot of these events, think about volunteering to work at the event to get yourself in the door for free. (Staffing the registration table is a great way to see who's attending so you can identify the people you want to meet later.) Once you're there, scan the room and look for the people you want to meet. You'll probably also meet other people you should know for your network, too, even if you weren't looking for them.
- *Build in an extra day for meetings when you travel* for professional purposes (or even on vacations) in or near towns with important people and organizations, such as Washington, D.C., or a state capital. Set up short meetings with people you want to know. People are much more willing to take a chance on a meeting with some unknown academic if you go to them.

While it might seem daunting to take this on, if you reach out in at least some of these ways, your network will grow and will connect you to the people you need to know. If the thought of adding new tasks to your already busy life fills you with dread, remember that this will happen over time. Developing a network is the project for a career, not for one summer or a semester. Networks made it possible for psychologist David P. Barash and psychiatrist Judith Lipton to get their book *The Caveman and the Bomb* into the hands of one of the most powerful people in the world, but their networks didn't grow overnight. Use your time well, though, and you can create an effective network more efficiently and can put it to work when you need it.

Make It Easy for Them

Thinking about your future network is a good reminder of some other useful principles related to your networking. Everybody is busy! So you also need to respect the busy lives of the people in your evolving network. Here are a few more suggestions for planning your interactions with your network members. These overlap a bit with communications skills that I'll discuss in the next three chapters, but mainly they connect some of the future discussions to the specific question of networking.

1. *Make it easy for people to see your value.* Don't send a long article without including an "executive summary" (usually a very short summary of the main findings and recommendations from a larger study—but not your academic abstract) of the study. Better yet, craft a few sentences in the email summarizing the article and explicitly saying how your findings or ideas might be directly useful for the person you're writing to.
2. *Don't be afraid to try again if someone does not respond to your first email or phone call.* But don't be snarky about it, because

you're asking them to take time out of their busy schedule to think hard about how you fit into their world.

3. *Make a personal connection.* Listen to what they tell you in response to your question about how your work might be useful in some way. Ask follow-up questions if they use jargon that you don't understand. That will make it easier for them to do the same with you.

4. *Do not assume that they know about the work in your field (especially theory), but don't talk down to them about your academic work.* They aren't likely to care much about how innovative your work is in your academic world—their interests are almost always the issues they work on and how you fit in there.

5. *Practice explaining your work in nonacademic language.* Find a friend in a totally different field to start your practice. Then explain it to a nonacademic partner or neighbor. Try your parents or grandparents. Work on different versions, including the "elevator speech"—what you'd say to the head of an organization or a member of Congress if you suddenly found yourself face-to-face with his or her undivided attention for a thirty-second ride between floors. Your elevator speech should succinctly explain how what you know is important for the person you're talking to. Even if you don't find yourself in those situations, it's good to have something to say to someone lower down the decision-making food chain that you're cultivating as a network contact.

Building Relationships for Strong Ties

The point of networking is to give us a means to get the knowledge and perspectives that we've developed into the public realm and to be a part of the change process. We want to be useful, but it's important to remember that usefulness is in the eye of the beholder. For example, you might think that your contribution is your analysis of new public opinion poll data that reveals a better way to frame a particular issue to appeal to the most voters. But the people in the campaign you want to influence might look at you and see someone who can work with numbers and make sense of their own voter database. In other words, your Power-Point presentation of findings, however lovingly adorned with clever graphics, might not be what that campaign needs or can process. You can find another audience—or you can roll up your sleeves and help out with the task at hand, holding off on your own ideas till the time is ripe.

A common theme among engaged scholars is that they often get started in building an important new relationship by doing work that isn't necessarily highly valued on a professional level. Melissa Michelson's white paper for practitioners was a good example of a young scholar taking a risk to produce something that is valued more highly outside than inside the academy. She used that experience to build stronger relationships that led to some academic publications later.

Sometimes that search for mutual advantage is more explicit and immediate. Some scholars' experience with the old-fashioned "I'll help you if you help me" shows that we can build strong relationships with organizations outside of academia that both sides will directly benefit from.[13] Political scientist Andra Gillespie developed exactly that kind of relationship with Cory Booker, when he was making his first run as a mayoral candidate in Newark, New Jersey. In 2002, Gillespie tested the effectiveness of different kinds of voter canvassing on turnout, providing some much-needed volunteer labor to Booker's campaign (he lost, but was successful four years later). In return, Gillespie not only got data for her dissertation, but she got some new ideas and connections that gave her access to data for a larger book project.

Organizational needs and the ability to find a mutual interest aren't the only issues to consider. Size and resources might matter in organizations' ability and willingness to work with you. A small organization that has few resources might potentially gain a lot from your volunteer help, but the time their staff would have to commit plus the risk that you won't follow through could tip the balance toward not working with you. (We often see this dynamic with students who enthusiastically approach local organizations with community-service learning ideas.) Larger organizations might have more capacity to work with a new person but might want you to do projects that seem less central to the organization or to your interests.

Also, building relationships will mean getting beyond the stereotypes that we might have about people in those other locations. The research on the use of science in policymaking is full of theories about how researchers and policymakers come from "two cultures" (or more), making communication and working together difficult.[14] Bogenschneider and Corbett talked to researchers who had built relationships with policymakers and grew to respect them for their dedication, idealism, hard work, and public spirit. They suggest that researchers become "biculturally competent" to have successful and satisfying interactions with the policy process by understanding the context, values, political processes, communication practices, time demands, and political incentives faced by policymakers.[15]

Your initial contribution to building a long-term valuable relationship might take a variety of forms. You might offer consulting services, volunteer work, editing services, or something else. If you can get in the door, collaborating on a relatively low-stakes, achievable goal is an excellent way to build trust and a stronger relationship with an important person or organization. The point is that stronger ties might result in stronger networks over the long haul, and your offers of help to demonstrate your usefulness might be your path to more intensive engagement related to your own research.

Tending and Weeding Your Network of Weaker Ties

In addition to the work you'll do to build certain key relationships, there are other ways to maintain and tend your growing garden of contacts. It's rare that a contact would be culled and tossed aside, especially if you've invested a lot in the relationship, but over time you'll get a sense of which contacts need the most nurturing and what kind of nurturing works best. Keeping in touch is an art form. Some people are naturally good at it, while the rest of us have to learn from their example.

From time to time take a look at the big picture. If you've mapped out some network locations, fill in the names of individuals in each location. You can see where you're strong and where you could do better, particularly if you want or need to move in a new direction.

As with our gardens and retirement accounts, diversifying your network is a good idea. Rapid changes in the media industry mean that the journalist who interviewed you about a study one year ago is gone or reassigned the next time you've got a study to promote. Also, organizations working in the same area do not always talk to each other, so knowing a lot of people in organization X doesn't mean that people in related organization Y have ever heard your name. Worse yet, occasionally an organization will see their networks—and perhaps you—as assets to be hoarded rather than shared. But you will be most effective as a shared public resource if you have ties across organizational borders.

The most important thing to do is to keep in touch. Your own personal listserv announcing a new study is probably less useful than a personalized greeting in an individual email and a message tailored to a specific person's needs. If you know something is brewing on your issue, offer to help out in some way. Even if you aren't seen as being needed, your contacts will appreciate your offer and might remember you when they really do need you.

If someone asks for help, try to be helpful. While that might seem obvious, sometimes the help they need isn't in our particular areas of expertise. If you have a good scholarly network, you might suggest they reach out to a specific person. But you might also know enough to sketch out what some of the issues are in another area—and if you don't, that's something you might want to look into. As this book argues, you'll be more effective if you know something about the big picture, and often that level of knowledge is sufficient.

With a growing and flexible network, you will be well positioned to hear about opportunities to get involved in public debates, and you will be ready to get involved and be useful. Gary Orfield's long career attests to the power of networks for engaged scholars:

> Life in a policy stream is unpredictable. . . . Sometimes a chance conversation at a meeting or an interview for a newspaper article leads to an important idea, while research requiring a year of serious work disappears without a trace. It is important to network broadly, interact continually with people in the field, be willing to participate in events of little apparent value, respond to media inquiries, and be ready to

seize unexpected opportunities. Networks often open up important opportunities.[16]

Your network will help you get your ideas and research into the hands of the people who need them and can use them. Your network contacts can hold your hand if times get rough. And your network will give you feedback and ideas that will make your research better. A strong network is a valuable and amazing resource for engaged scholars. Cultivate it, maintain it, and use it wisely, and it will bear fruit for many years.

5

Communicating outside of the Academy

"Is a 13-year-old girl selling sex on the streets a criminal?" asked lawyer and women's studies professor Carrie Baker.[1] In her research on human trafficking laws, Baker came across many cases of young girls who were arrested and convicted of prostitution in the United States, while their adult male customers and pimps went unpunished. If these girls had been brought here from other countries, they would have been seen as sexually exploited rather than criminals. Baker's law degree and a Ph.D. in women's studies gave her the scholarly skills to write law review articles that show how "safe harbor laws" are a better approach, providing social services for these exploited girls instead of prosecuting them. But she also wanted to reach a wider audience. Her transition to writing for a more popular audience wasn't easy, though.

"Academics obviously write like academics. Journalism is very, very different," Baker noted in an interview with *The Chronicle of Higher Education*. A workshop offered to women's studies faculty by *Ms.* magazine opened the door for Baker, where the challenges became clearer. "As an academic, you get so in your rut of writing 50-word sentences. I think it was really good for me as a scholar to kind of say, Let's bring this to a level where it can be popularly consumed."

Coming out of the workshop, Baker wrote an article for *Ms.* on the prosecution of young girls for prostitution. Stepping outside of academia got her publicly engaged in a big way, both in and out of the spotlight. The article won a national journalism award and led to television appearances and public speaking opportunities for Baker. Advocates circulated copies of her article to every Ohio state legislator as they considered a bill that would stop the prosecution of minors for prostitution and provide services for the young women instead. People emailed her with more horror stories about girls who had been prosecuted, and she matched up those stories with local activists who were trying to change conditions for those girls in specific cities.

Baker had something to say, and she found a way to convince people to listen. Once they listened, people began to use her research in their efforts for change.

Once you know what you want to say and who should be listening, it's time to communicate by using the media and other opportunities opened up by your network. Maybe you've heard an academic colleague interviewed on NPR, or read their op-ed in the *New York Times*. Maybe you've imagined yourself in the same position, inserting your own voice in the wider public conversation about your field of research.

To be influential, you don't have to limit your aspirations to the *New York Times*. Even for well-known public intellectuals, "[i]t is easier to win a lottery than to get [an op-ed] into the *New York Times*."[2] Fortunately, we live in a technologically remarkable era that makes it possible to reach the entire world with a single blog post—at least in theory. The tools are there for scholars to engage with the public directly, if we know how to use them. Effective communication plus a well-developed network give you the means to reach deep into the institutions that make decisions that affect us all.

Making that equation add up is not as simple as learning new software, though. This chapter and the next two present three kinds of tools to help you communicate better with journalists, policymakers, and community organizations in lots of new writing genres. (As a side benefit, your academic writing will probably improve, too.) First, in this chapter, come the most obvious skills, mainly clarity in writing and speaking to different audiences. Some less well-known tools get at the often hidden side of communication: framing your message and appealing to your audience in ways that will facilitate your communication goals. Both pieces together constitute the kind of strategic communication that is at the heart of influential engagement.

But First, a Word From Your Audience

The subtitle of a book by Frank Luntz, a communications guru for American conservatives, neatly sums up the communication challenge: *It's Not What You Say, It's What People Hear.* And what do others hear when scholars speak? Jargon.

At a retirement party for my colleague Arlene Avakian, chair of our Women, Gender, and Sexuality Studies Department, our state representative, Ellen Story, presented Arlene with a well-deserved resolution passed by the state legislature. Representative Story read the impressive document to the crowd, with laudatory "whereas clauses" (common to legislation) noting Arlene's many contributions, including this one: "Whereas, Professor Avakian has displayed an unwavering commitment to interdisciplinary and intersectional analysis in her career . . ."

At the mention of the word "intersectional," a surprised buzz shot through the audience of humanities scholars and social scientists: Could it be that they finally get it? That policymakers now understand the importance of seeing how the influences of race, gender, and sexuality intersect to create complex patterns of inequality? After she reached the end of the long sentence, Ellen paused, looking up to add with an impish smile, "You can tell that this wording came from the university—the legislature would *never* use the word 'intersectional'!"

Of course we laughed, but we also squirmed a bit in the face of more evidence that we don't talk the way other people do—and that's a big problem if we want to be relevant and engaged. Academics invest a lot of time and effort in creating theories about the world and the terms specific to those theories. We need that vocabulary, or jargon, when we talk to each other in our fields.

When I was a graduate student, a visiting scholar from another country asked me to provide feedback on a paper he was writing in my field of labor economics. I quickly saw that his written English was almost impossible to follow, to put it mildly. Even so, I gradually realized that I *could* understand what he was saying. On one profound level, we spoke the same language, the language of labor economics, and that was enough to give me the context to understand what he was trying to say.

While our jargon gives us almost a universal language within our fields, it's the biggest barrier to communication with people outside of the university. Back in the 1990s, Michael Warner, now a professor at Yale, criticized the media attention focused on a set of conservative gay male writers, while he saw exciting ideas from queer theorists being left out of the wider public mix of ideas.[3] On thinking about Warner's argument at the time, I was struck by the fact that the conservative gay men he critiqued were all professional journalists, while the queer theorists were, well, theorists. Was the lack of attention to the queer theorists a result of their political stance or their theoretical jargon that no one else could understand?

Maybe the two are related—oppositional politics and new theoretical terms. One of the people Warner wanted to hear more from in the public realm is Judith Butler, the noted philosopher on the political left. Butler is often picked on by the media and even by other academics for her dense prose. She defended her writing style in a *New York Times* op-ed essay:

> If common sense sometimes preserves the social status quo, and that status quo sometimes treats unjust social hierarchies as natural, it makes good sense on such occasions to find ways of challenging common sense. Language that takes up this challenge can help point the way to a more socially just world.[4]

Even in her defense of theoretical language, Butler at least acknowledged the need to translate and be clear. Her essay itself is proof that even theorists can be clear (or at least clearer) for those not steeped in the world of theory that she inhabits.

It's certainly possible for those on the left (and right) to write accessible and even entertaining prose. For example, Paul Krugman won a Nobel Prize in economics for his work in international economic theory, mainly communicated in articles full of equations, graphs, and statistics. He's got the theoretical credibility of Butler in his own field, but he also manages to write a very popular *New York Times* column that my nonacademic friends on the left love to quote. Krugman is a great example of an engaged and influential scholar who would not be so influential if he couldn't communicate effectively to noneconomists.

For other public speaking examples of academics who communicate well to nonacademic audiences, I recommend TED talks on "Ideas Worth Spreading." One of the keys to successful TED talks is a lack of jargon.[5]

The key point to keep in mind is that our audience will be the judge of our clarity. I am not saying that we should dump our theoretical language. We need it when we're communicating with other scholars in our fields. However, almost every other audience would like for us to stop using unfamiliar terms and to explain the strange terms that we insist are really important to use. This is probably not surprising advice, and it's certainly not original—but it is the most important place to start.

The Basics: Messages and Talking Points

Messages: Clarify, Simplify, Amplify, Repeat

At this stage, I will assume that you have some audiences in mind as well as a sense of what your contribution to a particular public debate might be. Now it's time to hone that contribution into a message in terms that will resonate with your audience. A message plus some talking points provides a strong base for a variety of communication options, so it's worth investing a little time to come up with some messages from your own ideas.

What's a message? A message is the core argument or claim that you want some audience to accept, believe, or learn. It's the point you want someone to get. In Frank Luntz's words, it's what you want your audience to hear.

A message is not the same thing as a sound bite, although having a bite-sized version of your message can be very valuable in many contexts. If you can put your message into just a few words or a memorable sentence or phrase, you can fit it into pretty much any context.

In academia, we would call the message a "thesis." Amitai Etzioni describes an influential message he has circulated for two decades in just this way: "Hence, the thesis that my fellow communitarians and I raised—that individual rights were paramount, but so were social responsibilities—was rather well received by the public."[6] Etzioni uses terms with complex meanings here, which is not surprising given that he was writing for an audience of political scientists at the time. The succinctness of his message is what makes it possible to circulate widely, although probably in somewhat different terms, such as (in my very plain words), "Individuals should have basic rights in our society, but individuals also have social responsibilities."

The main thing to notice in the examples in Box 5.1 is that these are very simple and fairly short in my formulation. There's an underlying "should" in each one, since these messages point to the need for some kind of action, and there's an implicit counterargument to a few. These messages don't relate to a single study or the work of one scholar. Also, note that all of these messages are centered on a public discussion or debate, not academic theory. They aren't simple ideas (some might even say these messages are too complex), but they are simply stated.

These messages also vary. Some are more contextual, others more specific. Some are messages coming from a lifetime of work, others from a recent study. A message is pretty much the same thing as a "take-home point" or "the takeaway," to borrow the title of a popular public radio show.

We often hear the term "staying on message"—a reminder to speakers to avoid distracting arguments or uncomfortable changes

Box 5.1. Messages Related to Academic Work

Here are some examples of very plain messages that relate to academic work:

- To end poverty, we need to create more good jobs and improve access to those jobs.
- Medical use of marijuana can safely relieve pain, nausea, and other symptoms of serious illnesses.
- An independent special prosecutor should be appointed to investigate police officers who are accused of using excessive force.
- Mass incarceration has contributed to disenfranchisement and impoverishment of African Americans in the U.S.
- Paid family leave would be good for children and would help parents balance career and family issues.
- Environmental damage hurts everyone, but people of color bear more of that cost than white Americans.
- Reducing greenhouse gas emissions and promoting renewable energy won't hurt the economy—in fact, it will create more jobs.
- Cutting funding for public universities will lead to higher tuition for students and put an end to the middle-class American dream of affordable education for all.

in topic. In the mouth of a flustered politician, staying on message can lead to repetition and evasion of tough questions.

In my experience, however, staying on message is both a flexible guideline and a good reminder to keep coming back to what you want the audience to learn, even as you listen carefully and respond to questions with more detailed answers. From the communications world, Scott Swenson puts it nicely: "Staying on message should not turn someone into a robot; it is a rudder with which to steer your way through an argument/interview." Once you have a strong and clear message, you've got the most important tool for reaching a wide variety of audiences.

Creating Your Own Message

Now the key question: What's *your* message? If you can see the big picture in the area you're working in after a review of the debate, then you have probably found some places that your ideas or knowledge fit in. Those are probably the best places to start developing a message. Over time, you will probably work on many messages, but just start with one.

With the audience you want to reach in mind, hone your idea into a message using two key principles:

1. *Clarify*: Keep it jargon free.
2. *Simplify*: Keep it short and relatively simple.

My earlier rant against jargon is probably sufficient to convey the first point. Take the ideas or empirical knowledge that you want to contribute to the debate. Write it down. Edit any jargon out. At this point, you've got something like this example from Box 5.1: Reducing greenhouse gas emissions and promoting renewable energy won't hurt the economy—in fact, it will create more jobs.

Then draw on Thoreau's famous life advice: "Simplify, simplify." You don't need a hundred thousand words to convey a powerful message or two. Simplify, hack, trim, and shape those ideas into messages that are relevant and meaningful to the realm you're entering. Think poetry, not essay.

- Saving our planet will be good for the economy.
- We will strengthen our environment and our economy by producing renewable energy.
- Being good stewards of the earth will pay off with stronger economies.

- We can stabilize an already-changing climate in a way that promotes economic prosperity.[7]

Then consider the context and the hidden meanings you're expressing. What images does your draft message convey? What images might tap into your audience's logic, values, or emotions? The examples above aren't sophisticated, well-tested messages, but they can give you some sense of how certain words may sound. "Prosperity" might have wide appeal across different political perspectives. "Stewardship" might evoke religious values, perhaps a good thing for your audience. "Stabilization" suggests the need for an active response to change.

Rewrite your message several different ways. Read each version out loud. How does it make you feel to say it to an imaginary audience? Which audiences do you imagine for different versions?

Try them out. Short of organizing a focus group, you can get valuable feedback by trying out different versions on different people (including people from the network you're developing). See how they respond to one version. What do they ask you about? Do they seem to agree? What does their body language or tone of voice tell you? Do they think about it or respond instinctively? Which versions seem to get the effect you hoped for? If you're offering some new twist on an old idea, one of Frank Luntz's "ten rules of effective language," you might hear people respond, "I didn't know that," a good response in this context.

Use a group of nonacademics (or at least people who aren't in your field) for a game of "message telephone," something I've used in workshops. Tell one person your favorite or best version of your message. Then ask them to tell another person the message they took away. The second person repeats what he or she heard as your key point to the third person, etc. If this mini–focus group is all in one room as you do this, you'll see the power of repetition to reinforce your message, since the last person has the advantage of hearing all who came before. If you separate the people, though, you'll get a more powerful read on your ability to communicate your message well. If "Saving our planet will be good for the economy" turns into "Saving your money is good for retirement," then start over!

Revise your message. Repeat and revise again.

Academics get hung up on creating a message because we feel like we must take ownership of it. However, *your message does not have to be your own unique creation or contribution.*

In fact, it usually makes sense to use messages that are similar or even the same as the ones that others working in your area are using. If you've tracked the debate and have sketched out the beginnings of a network, you've probably already encountered more than one message that's relevant to your work. Try to identify those messages, and pay attention to how they're used. (I return to this question of how messages are framed below.) Those messages are probably out there because they relate to popular concerns or sentiments and are at least perceived to be powerful influences on people's beliefs. Also, using existing messages makes your work more relevant to the other people in the debate.

The other big advantage of linking to an existing message is that repetition is the key to being heard. Aaron Belkin points to the power of repeated and consistent research findings in undermining the foundations of the Don't Ask Don't Tell policy, not just in the minds of academics, but in public opinion and policymakers' opinions.[8] While we value novel ideas and innovation in academia, widespread learning happens through repetition of a message, both for our students and our larger audiences. Your own individual contribution to a message is more likely to come in the talking points and the support for those talking points.

Add Talking Points

Now you need talking points. These talking points are the backbone of your message. They might be simple pieces of reasoning, facts, stories, or even a few details of potential policies, but they should all directly support your message. You might have a couple of sets of talking points to relate to more than one message, or to bolster different components. Each one should be short, usually no more than a sentence—two at most.

Talking points are extremely helpful in a couple of ways. As their name implies, they provide great notes and reminders to review before talking to a journalist, meeting with a policymaker, or going on a radio show. They might provide an outline for an op-ed essay. You can share them with others who want to use your argument. You can also assess the feedback you get on the different points and adjust accordingly, adding, subtracting, or revising.

Box 5.2 provides some talking points for one of the messages that I listed earlier: We can stabilize an already-changing climate in a way that promotes economic prosperity.

Where did those talking points come from? Each one responds to points that come up in the public debate, and the sources are scientists like Ray Bradley and the Intergovernmental Panel on Climate Change.[9] The third set of talking points are conclusions drawn from a study by Robert Pollin, Heidi Garrett-Peltier, James Heintz, and Bracken Hendricks.[10] So the talking points speak to one team's research study and draw on other scholars' findings from a variety of disciplines. Further detail could be fleshed out with those studies if necessary.

Box 5.2. Examples of Talking Points on Climate Change and the Economy

1. *We can stabilize . . . the climate . . .:*

   a. Human activities, mainly the burning of fossil fuels, have caused climate change.

   b. Reducing greenhouse gas emissions so that by 2050 we're emitting 40% to 70% below 2010 levels could help contain global warming to two degrees Celsius. These reductions would reduce the likelihood of irreversible climate change.

2. *. . . an already-changing climate . . .:* Scientists have found clear evidence of climate change, including rising global temperatures, rising sea levels, and changes in local ecosystems.

3. *. . . in a way that promotes economic prosperity:*

   a. Without action, climate change will lead to extreme weather events and other extremely harmful effects on the economy.

   b. With an annual investment of $200 billion by private and public entities, the U.S. could meet emissions goals by increasing energy efficiency and producing energy through low- or zero-emissions renewable energy sources.

   c. The cost of such investments could be covered through a carbon tax.

   d. Even taking into account jobs lost in fossil fuels industries, the U.S. would see 2.7 million net new jobs created with such a plan.

Since the message and talking points are useful in so many contexts, put some effort into refining them. (They're almost always a work in progress.) Try them out on friends and colleagues to see if they make sense. Practice them. Memorize them so you're ready to pull them out whenever you have an opportunity.

Everyone Has a Message

On first glance, this kind of approach obviously works well for a social scientist whose expertise leads to talking points related to a message. The climate change example shows that other messages might easily be rooted in the physical sciences, followed by accessible talking points that support and extend that claim. I would argue that all fields are useful for generating messages relevant to public audiences.

While engagement that taps into our professional knowledge is the main activity I'm discussing in this book, we have many other reasons to get involved in public debates. We're all citizens with a stake in public debates and public decisions. As journalism professor Robert Jensen puts it, "Experts sometimes have important contributions to make to such public debates. Citizens *always* have such contributions" (emphasis added).[11] The message-plus-talking-points formula is a powerful one for any issue we're engaged with, regardless of whether it taps into your own research area or you are responding as a citizen.

One of the good things about being clear on your own message is that you don't have to know everything about an issue to make a difference. Your message is your main angle or contribution, and you can pull conversations back to it when you need to. Stay open to other messages that might emerge from your experiences in the debate, and think about ways to refine and improve the messages you use and hear. Messages evolve over time because people and debates evolve.

Framing: The Message behind the Words

In the political world, a message is both a means and an end. Much research goes into defining and refining messages, going well beyond achieving the goal of jargon-free clarity to figuring out the most persuasive way to frame or present messages. "Messaging" is a subject of study all its own. Pollsters will test messages to see which ones work best in focus groups or opinion surveys to achieve the result that a client wants. Politicians look for messages that will win over voters. Social movements want messages that change public hearts and minds. Lawyers want messages that will sway juries and judges. They're all looking for the way to present a message that will hold an audience's attention and engage their hearts and minds in a reconsideration of their opinions and beliefs.[12]

The presentation of a message is what is known as "framing." Sociologist Steve Boutcher studies social movements, and he teaches his students that a message frame is like a window frame. By directing your eye, the window shapes what you're allowed to see, blocking some things and revealing others. Linguist George Lakoff, who interprets framing from the left end of the ideological spectrum, calls frames "mental structures that shape the way we see the world."[13]

Our brains interpret words and arguments in ways that fit our worldview, or the moral values that guide us. Frank Luntz tells conservatives to talk about "tax relief" instead of "tax cuts," for example. "Tax relief" sounds like a deserved break for overburdened taxpayers, while "tax cuts" are often promised but rarely delivered. Likewise, "drilling for oil" calls to mind images of oil rigs that sometimes have horrific leaks, while "exploring for energy" suggests heroic efforts with clean, innovative technologies to fuel the economy.

Luntz's advice reflects what Lakoff calls a "strict father" view of the world, where taxes punish disciplined people who are living good, moral lives and redistribute their money to undeserving people. Liberals, in contrast, are more likely to have a "nurturant parent" model of the world, where taxes are seen as reasonable contributions to ensure the provision of government services.

For academics who want to inject new facts or new perspectives into a public conversation, understanding frames is crucial. Communication experts from both the left and right understand this point. Lakoff argues, "To be accepted, the truth must fit people's frames. If the facts do not fit a frame, the frame stays and the facts bounce off."[14] Luntz advises his clients similarly, as seen in a memo to conservatives: "Facts only become relevant when the public is receptive and willing to listen to them."[15]

Good organizers who want to create change understand this point, too. Saul Alinksy's *Rules for Radicals* has a whole chapter on communication. Alinsky's main point in that chapter fits the Lakoff and Luntz perspectives: "People only understand things in terms of their experience, which means that you must get within their experience."[16]

To some, framing might seem manipulative, a tool of propaganda. As Lakoff puts it, "Reframing *is* social change."[17] And yet the frames themselves already exist. Anytime we use language to represent or convey ideas, we are using some kind of frame, whether we are conscious of it or not. Our academic theories create frames for our research. If we aren't conscious of the scientific frames we're using to communicate research about climate change, for example, we're not communicating effectively with our audience members whose values include questioning scientific authority. If we don't use these insights about framing, we're leaving it to other people to determine how our research gets interpreted in a public debate.

Also, there is no framing formula for communication that will magically make people agree with us. In my view, effective communication means getting people to consider our ideas and research seriously and carefully, not necessarily to agree with us. The quality of an idea still matters. Luntz points out (and Lakoff acknowledges) that all the careful framing in the world won't make up for a bad or unpopular idea. Nevertheless, the point of framing is that good ideas will have more life and power when framed in a way that fits the worldviews of the audience.

Using Framing for Research Findings

Unlike politicians and organizations, you probably won't do a poll or extensive research to frame your message, although over time your networking and sense of the big picture will help you understand how and why others working on your issue choose the frames they use. Our research constantly uses frames, whether we are conscious of them or not, and sometimes a helpful contribution you might make is to add a new frame.

While quantitative researchers tend to see our quantities as objective measures, even numbers are framed.[18] Consider some numbers in the debate about outlawing discrimination against lesbian, gay, bisexual, and transgender people with a federal civil rights law. Opponents of such laws routinely demand evidence of a problem. In response, scholars have counted the number of formal complaints about actual cases of discrimination in states that ban it. But the opponents unfailingly offer at least one of these framings of the exact same numbers:

1. The numbers are *so small* that it's clear discrimination isn't a problem that warrants a policy change.
2. The numbers are *so big* that this is clearly evidence that employers will be burdened by defending themselves in lawsuits.

Legal scholar Bill Rubenstein labeled these two seemingly irreconcilable interpretations the "drought" and the "flood" arguments, two vivid frames.[19]

Then he offered an alternative framing. Instead of looking at the raw counts of complaints, look at the proportion of LGBT people who actually file complaints. That proportion looks very similar to the proportion of women and people of color who file sex or race discrimination complaints in the same states. In other words, the sexual orientation complaints are neither a drought nor a flood. They're not too big; they're not too small. The figures we see are what we'd expect given the degree of discrimination in our labor market.

Engaged scholars can also use some insights from research on framing. One very important implication of the framing literature is that exposure to clearly presented research findings about a complex problem or project is not enough to convince the general public to change their opinions or to act on scientific research. While clarity is a virtue in communication, reaching people with research requires presenting findings more strategically.

A group of scholars involved in the Cultural Cognition Project at Yale University conducted experiments to measure the impact of research on public opinion among a wide range of controversial topics, such as gun control, climate change, adoption by gay parents, and the use of nanotechnology.[20] The experiments asked whether research findings actually change public opinion. The bad news is that the research confirms Lakoff's point: People mainly believe research findings that support their existing beliefs about the world, and findings that are inconsistent with beliefs can lead to a hardening of positions on controversial topics. The good news is that research can influence opinion, but effective communication takes planning and thought on our parts.

Consider the issue of whether gay and lesbian couples should be allowed to adopt children. Overall, 58% of individuals surveyed by the project at least mildly agreed that gay couples should be able to adopt kids.[21] About half of the people surveyed said that the impact on child welfare was the most important reason for their opinions, whether for or against gay adoption. The study then presented respondents with findings from fictional studies that showed gay parents having either positive or negative effects on the welfare of adopted kids, but reading those findings had very little effect on respondents' opinions about the issue.

One reason the research didn't budge opinions seems to be that people filter research through their existing beliefs and opinions. When respondents were presented with conflicting findings from similar (fictional) research studies on the impact on child welfare, they rated the study that supported their existing cultural beliefs as being of higher quality than the study that contradicted their beliefs. The researchers have seen people reject research findings that threaten their values in the other issues they have studied, too.[22]

Armed with that knowledge, the authors offer some helpful lessons for more effective communication by engaged scholars. First, to get an audience to pay careful attention to credible research that conflicts with their preexisting views, we should present findings in a way that fits into a listener's value system. The Cultural

---

Box 5.3. Finding Frames That Work

Several sources of information and ideas about framing are publicly available.

- The FrameWorks Institute (www.frameworksinstitute.org) is a nonprofit organization that is "changing the conversation on social issues" by using research to help nonprofits frame their work more effectively. Their work covers a wide range of environmental, immigration, criminal justice, health, education, and social issues.

- The Cultural Cognition Project at Yale (www.culturalcognition.net) studies the impact of values on policy beliefs, particularly those related to science and technology. The project's blog often explores cutting-edge scholarship on the science of communicating science.

- The National Academies of Science conducted a symposium on "The Science of Science Communication" in 2012, and talks and panels are available online: http://www.nasonline.org/programs/sackler-colloquia/completed_colloquia/agenda-science-communication.html.

Cognition Project results point to two dimensions of values that matter for many controversial issues: the range from egalitarian to authoritarian (that is, the extent to which people have a preference for traditional social hierarchies) and from individualistic to communitarian. When research subjects saw messages and a messenger that were aligned with their own values, they were more likely to focus on, understand, and sometimes to accept research findings on controversial issues.

An extension of that point is that we should present findings in different ways to appeal to different audiences. Research findings that affirm different values might appeal to a much wider range of people, and these different presentations give us the opportunity to get more people to think carefully about what we've learned.

The second lesson is that researchers can effectively use "vouching," or the presentation of research findings by trusted messengers, as a strategy for affecting options. Vouching draws on the power of networks by getting our research in the hands of people who have credibility and connections with people whose values might differ from our own. Our academic credibility is an asset and makes us good messengers in some situations, usually with policymakers and the media. But the cultural cognition research shows that members of the general public are more open to messengers who reflect their values. Sometimes those users of your research will also be "validators," who attest to the value and credibility of your ideas and findings.

The cultural cognition work also suggests that messengers who use research to express surprising positions to people of a particular value system are especially powerful and might even contribute to the convergence of polarized positions. In the gays-in-the-military debate, Belkin used surprising validators, such as retired generals and admirals, to carry research findings into the public realm.[23]

Handing off our ideas to other messengers might seem risky. One of the hardest things for scholars is letting go of control over their own ideas and research findings. My idealistic advice is to do the communications work discussed here, and then set your ideas and findings free! Let them take on a life of their own, putting them in front of people who can appreciate their value. Those other messengers will pick them up and make them persuasive to audiences that would never pay attention to or believe an ivory tower professor. If messengers use or express ideas in ways that aren't exactly what you would do or say, you can contact them and give them feedback, or use other options to correct or extend their presentation of the ideas. But usually that won't be necessary.

Your work will reach more deeply into the public realm and into the hearts and minds of your audiences if you communicate strategically, using clear messages and appropriate messengers. The next two chapters show you how to further amplify the influence of your ideas and findings, tucked into a message, into different communication channels.

6

Using Traditional Media Outlets to Connect with the World

· · · · · · · · · · · · · · · · · · ·

American parents are shocked to learn from sociologist Amy Schalet that Dutch parents let their teenagers invite a boyfriend or girlfriend over to spend the night. Schalet's research shows big cross-cultural differences in how parents address their teens' sexuality. Americans parents worry about their teens' raging hormones and the risks of sexual activity; Dutch parents talk to their kids about building good relationships.[1]

That sharp contrast probably explains why Schalet got her own nickname in the U.S. media, "the sleepover sociologist," even before she got tenure. She has reached potentially millions of ordinary people through radio interviews, newspaper reviews, and her op-eds in the *Washington Post* and the *New York Times* on teenagers' sexuality. Schalet also shares her research with pediatricians and other professionals who work with young people and need new strategies for dealing with adolescent sexuality.

While Amy's research had a great hook, it also risked turning off broader audiences. So she centered her message on the importance of good relationships—between parents and teens, and between young people—to produce a takeaway point that audiences could embrace.

Once Amy had that message, she found many ways to reach widespread audiences. Likewise, once you're clear on your own message, get it out into the world. If you've thought about the playing field and have begun to sketch out your ideal network, you've got ideas and some options for places to send your message. With practice, you'll be ready for any opportunity. Your message gets amplified from a whisper out of your computer, into a quiet conversation with others, then a louder buzz, finally echoing across many groups of people and places.

Your message and talking points are the keys to communicating with just about any audience. What might those audiences look like? They won't just look like your colleagues, and you won't reach them in the same way. The first column in Box 6.1 lists the various outlets for writing about your research for your disciplinary colleagues. It's a familiar list, and very specialized (think jargon).

The experiences of Amy Schalet and other scholars you see in the media show the promise for reaching a much broader audience in using a longer list of writing and speaking genres, found in the second column of Box 6.1. From interviews with journalists, to blog posts and op-ed pieces, scholars have many options to reach new audiences. Not all of those options involve writing—as we've seen, policymakers often prefer to get their information through presentations or direct interactions with experts.[2] This chapter focuses on reaching traditional media and communication outlets, such as newspapers, radio, and specific policy forums. The next chapter takes on social media and the ability to rapidly disseminate your ideas in new ways.

Each of those outlets in the second column comes with its own institutional norms and customs. This chapter offers some advice for using traditional media from a range of scholars experienced in those arenas, including some of my own tips. That advice is

Box 6.1. Different Audiences and Writing Outlets

Academic outlets	Nonacademic outlets
Journal articles	Magazine articles
Working papers	Books for the general public
Books or book chapters for scholars	Newspaper op-ed pieces
Conference proceedings	Radio or TV interviews
Conference presentations	Interviews by print journalists
Poster presentations	Blog posts
Invited talks or lectures	Q&A features in print or online
	Comments on web pages or blogs
	Tweets or Facebook posts
	Podcasts
	Short briefing papers on an issue
	Detailed policy reports
	In-person formal briefings of policy-makers or other officials
	Informal discussions with policymakers or other officials
	Testimony in court or legislative hearings
	Amicus ("friend of the court") briefs for lawsuits
	Expert witness reports or affidavits for lawsuits
	Press releases or press advisories
	Speeches to community groups

useful, though, only if you know what you want to say, and whom you want to hear it.

Some General Communications Ideas

Before digging into each new forum, in this section I offer a few generic suggestions for making your ideas and research more attractive and digestible for public audiences of any kind.

Finding a Hook

Finding an opportunity to use what you know is easier if you can connect your ideas and the new audience you're after. In the words of journalism, you want to find a "hook." Hooks are little bridges that connect what you know to something your audience is interested in. A good hook can turn a cold call to an op-ed editor or journalist, or to anyone else in your network, into a rapidly warming call.

For example, police killings—and protests over grand juries' decisions not to indict the police officers responsible—in Ferguson, Missouri, and Staten Island created a hook for a host of op-eds in 2014. Vesla Weaver used that hook in the *Baltimore Sun* to write about her research on the impact of mass incarceration in Baltimore. Jeremy Travis and Bruce Western used it in the *Boston Globe* to show how the criminal justice system as a whole is undermining racial justice.

Some other examples of tried-and-true hooks might give you an idea of what to look for:

- A holiday with some tie-in to your interests is approaching, like Labor Day (research on labor issues), the Fourth of July (ideas about democracy), April 15 (tax policy), Mother's Day, or Father's Day (research on families or gender). *Hook for blog posts, op-eds, and other popular journalism*

- A bill will be debated in your city council or state legislature. *Hook for op-eds, testimony, blog posts, policy briefings, policy reports, media outreach, and advocacy outreach*
- You have a new research study or book coming out with surprising findings on a topic in the news. *Hook for press release, blogs, tweets, op-eds, media outreach, advocacy outreach, policy briefings, policy reports, and public speaking events*
- You know that a high-profile study by another scholar or organization will soon be released. *Hook for blogs, op-eds, tweets, and press advisories*
- A decision in a big lawsuit is due to come out soon. *Hook for op-eds, blogs, tweets, and press advisories*
- Some highly visible and relevant event, like a visit of a foreign dignitary or a big protest march, is coming up. *Hook for op-eds, media outreach, and advocacy outreach*

The magic formula in fishing for attention is now more fleshed out: Take your message, talking points, and stories, tie them to a hook, and wait for a nibble. Better yet, dangle your bait in front of a particular fish, drawing from the network you're developing. You'll put this message in a familiar form: a media interview, an op-ed piece, a briefing paper summarizing your ideas, an extended discussion in a blog post, testimony before policymakers, or a presentation before a professional organization. You've got all you need with this framework to reach people in many different locations.

The Power of Repetition

Repetition is a powerful tool in communication. (Have I already mentioned this?) Cognitive scientists have found that hearing opinions many times generates familiarity with an argument, even if only a few people are expressing a particular opinion multiple times. Familiarity, in turn, can lead people to think there's a consensus about the point, and that it's therefore more likely than not to be true.[3]

This point matters for you in several ways. The most obvious is that you want your own message to be repeated, whether by you or others. This advice goes against the academic grain, which values uniqueness and novelty. But media interviews, op-eds, and other forms of direct connection with the public are opportunities to reinforce your message through repetition. Ideally, members of your network are also repeating your message in other settings.

Maybe less obviously, you also want to be careful about repeating messages or ideas that conflict with your own. You want the first big message that people hear in a talk, radio show, or media interview to be yours. You have an idea or finding that you want to convey. Lead with that, not with the conventional wisdom or other research findings that you're contradicting. Stephanie Coontz's husband, a nonacademic, gave her this advice: "He said, 'Do not start with what somebody that you disagree with believes in academia. People will think that's what you believe.'" You can bring in other people's ideas, and it can enhance your credibility to point out why you're right and others are wrong, but make your point first and make that the one that people hear the most.

Memory Tools That (Sometimes) Work

Often we're engaging with new audiences because we think we've got some useful advice or knowledge for those groups. Your advice will be more meaningful if people can remember it. Even a simple memory tool or acronym will make it more likely that your ideas will stick in people's heads.

Psychologist Glenda Russell has become a therapist-to-a-social-movement in the LGBT rights field. She gives workshops based on her research into how people of all sexual orientations can deal with the fear, sadness, anger, and psychological trauma of living through anti-gay political campaigns. Glenda taps into sources of resilience for LGBT people and their allies.

Back in 2004, she summarized her work for a broader audience in a short paper.[4] She turned her initial discussion of resilience into "The Three As: Analysis, Action, and Allies." Having an understanding of why one might have bad reactions to the homophobia embedded in campaigns (the *analysis*), taking some kind of *action* to build community and resist homophobia, and tapping into supportive *allies* can all help LGBT people to cope and to grow in tough political times. Glenda still uses this approach in her workshops, and other psychologists and activists use her work with LGBT activists. They still use her short briefing paper, and they *always* mention the Three As as a useful tool. And as bad as my middle-aged memory has gotten, even I still remember them!

Amy Schalet has distilled her research on teenage sexuality into advice for parents, summarized in what she calls the "ABCD's of adolescent sexuality":[5]

- **A**utonomy—helping teenagers develop self-knowledge and take responsibility for their sexual lives
- **B**uilding healthy romantic relationships
- The **C**onnectedness of parents and children, including communication so that parents can continue to influence their teens
- Recognition of the **D**iversity of teenagers' development, sexual orientations, and cultural or religious beliefs

Schalet's use of the familiar ABCD format to summarize her advice gives her TV and radio audiences a fighting chance to remember at least some of it when they prepare to talk to their own teenagers.

Memory tools can be incredibly helpful for our audiences, even if they seem like gimmicks to us. Furthermore, the process of constructing these tools can also enhance our understanding of the useful pieces of research and the remaining gaps that we need to fill to link research and the real world.

Using Stories

Another tool for helping your audience understand and remember your research is to use stories about real people. Other research on communication, as well as best practice in the communications business, shows that stories increase the interest in your speaking or writing. I mentioned them in the last chapter as support for your talking points, perhaps making it sound like just another bullet point. But stories stand on their own and can be very valuable in many contexts, both in spoken media, like radio shows or public talks, and in written media, like op-eds. Even policymakers—make that, *especially* policymakers—love stories and will often match them skillfully with statistics.[6]

For example, you can use stories to spice up an op-ed piece. Robert Jensen tied a conversation with his young son into a compelling op-ed about sanctions against Iraq.[7] I've used stories from my friends' lives. In a *Boston Globe* op-ed on the so-called "marriage penalty" in the federal income tax, I told the story of close friends who got a big tax bill after getting married in a romantic, but ultimately expensive, gesture on New Year's Eve. Journalist Jim Tankersley used the history of the Huffy Bike company to tell a story about the deindustrialization of Ohio's economy for the *Washington Post*, and he says that even economists can tell stories to convey information. You can use a personal story, someone else's story that you have read about (lawsuits and newspaper articles are a great source of detailed and compelling stories), or any other anecdotes that help to make your point in vivid detail and trigger emotions that will increase your audience's receptiveness to your argument.

Usually the stories we know best are our own, and sometimes journalists will even ask whether you've experienced X (whatever your subject is). But if using your own story makes you uncomfortable, and it might if you work on topics that are highly personal or involve your family members, you can pivot away from such discussions by presenting a boring personal story and using it to bridge quickly into a more interesting one from another source.

Beware of Caveats

Pretty much every academic article I read in the social sciences has a section in it that outlines the limitations of the study: The sample size was small. The confidence intervals were large. The data aren't necessarily representative. The causal links are not clear. The measures are all self-reported and might not be accurate. Etc., etc.

The need to hedge comes naturally to us because of our professional scientific process and standards: We can never know with absolute certainty. I don't think we want to change that academic context, of course. In the larger world, though, I think it's safe to say that the caveats that academics use drive the media, and most other nonacademic users of research, crazy.

Fortunately, there's room to meet in the middle. We can publicly apply our professional judgment about the knowledge we gain from a body of research, drawing broad conclusions while acknowledging the subtleties. Stephanie Coontz understands both sides' needs and advises academics, "You can provide nuance, but stick it in the middle, not at the beginning or end" of an op-ed or discussion with a journalist. Geoscientist Ray Bradley takes a similarly practical approach: "But all political decisions have to be made on the basis of imperfect data; we rarely have all the facts, and this is obviously true as we try to anticipate how climate will change in the future."

Start noticing how often you add these caveats in talking with people outside of academia or in your writing for the public. Think about which ones are the most important, and try working them into a talking point to support your message without undermining it. If these caveats are not important in the formation of your own professional judgment, you should drop them from your communication practices.

Tips for Dealing with Different Communications Forums

Hooks, stories, and other memory tools are useful in all writing genres. The next few sections offer some tips and, in some cases, an introduction to a new set of gatekeepers for the ways to reach nonacademic audiences listed in Box 6.1.

Public Speaking

Starting back in elementary school, my own education included public speaking, and in high school my extracurricular activities included speech competitions and radio programs. I've usually enjoyed speaking in public. But when I started speaking in professional contexts after getting my Ph.D., I was nervous and unsure of myself, so I started writing out my comments in longer and longer forms and basically just read them in professional presentations. The result: I was boring, even when I was excited about my research.

Given the fact that our jobs require a lot of speaking to students and colleagues, you might think that academics would be great public speakers. Unfortunately, I think boring performances like my early ones are all too common among academics. The spoken word is a different genre from the written word, and good communicators will take note of that difference.

The excellent presenters I hear and have learned from put their research in a compelling package and present it engagingly, with lots of eye contact and without a script. They aren't reading from a paper, and they seem to be talking directly to me, even with hundreds of others in the audience. I follow those talks more closely and remember more than I did from someone reading a paper out loud.

We can all become more engaging speakers, no matter the context. To be more like the most effective presenters, wean yourself off of a scripted presentation, using shorter notes. Rehearse to make sure you meet time limits and feel comfortable looking at your audience. Craft a presentation that tells a story about your project—for example, why you felt compelled to study the topic, how you studied it, what you found, and especially, why those findings are important. Move around and show the audience the energy you feel.

Loosening up our speaking styles is absolutely essential for nonacademic audiences, whether to radio listeners or a live audience right in front of you. This point is about how you speak, not just what you're saying. You can certainly communicate complex arguments and ideas to nonacademic audiences, but you'd better

> ## Box 6.2. Tips for Public Speaking before Any Audience
>
> - Practice!
> - Have a narrative arc if you're giving a talk: a beginning, middle, and end.
> - Don't read a script!
> - Outline key takeaway points in notes, not a script.
> - Have links to transition between the points.
> - Tell a story.
> - If you're funny, be funny—but jokes are not necessary.
> - Make your message personal to your audience.
> - Keep your sentences short. (If you have to pause to breathe in the middle of a sentence, it's too long!)
> - Don't go over your time limit.
> - Memorize enough so you're making eye contact 80% of the time.

be ready to do it well. You need to grab an audience's attention and hold it until they understand and will remember your message.

You can find good advice about public speaking in many places. In my view, the best way to learn it is to do it and to get honest feedback from people you trust. No matter the context, preparation is key. In my experience, true extemporaneous speaking is rare. You almost always have time to prepare. Boxes 6.2 and 6.3 provide some guidelines that I've developed for my own public speaking. For some examples of lively and engaging (not to mention highly polished) talks about research and ideas, try TED.com.

Writing a Press Release or Press Advisory

Writing a press release isn't rocket science, but it's important when you have something new to announce. Press releases on research findings serve two purposes. First, a press release announces to the media that a new study has found some interesting and important findings and tries to convince those media to report on them. Second, many news websites will simply post all or a slightly edited version of press releases on related topics, so the press release also serves as a news story in and of itself.

Some universities have news offices with people to help faculty and students reach out to the news media. It's hard for them to write a good press release without your help though, especially if they are not familiar with your field or work. Even if someone in your university news office volunteers to draft a press release for you, you might want to draft some key parts, and you'll want a chance to edit it.

If you don't have someone to do this for you, then it's time to channel your inner journalist. Imagine the article you'd want someone to read on your study. This is your opportunity to present your findings to the public just the way you want to, unfiltered through a journalist's or editor's interpretation.

- Write "FOR IMMEDIATE RELEASE" at the top.
- Create a descriptive headline (aka title) that conveys the key message. You can elaborate a bit in a subheading.
- Include your contact information, usually your phone number and email address.

Box 6.3. Things to Remember about Speaking

- Make eye contact around the room.
- Warm up your voice beforehand.
- Relax so your voice drops.
- Vary your pacing.
- Use pauses to add drama or emphasis.
- Remember to breathe.

- Craft a lead sentence that grabs the reader's attention and conveys the key point of the study. Here you're presenting the conclusion, not the theoretical question, method, or other details of the study. Think about what is newsworthy about your study from the perspective of the news media, not other academics.
- Write in the third person.
- Provide quotes from the authors. The quotes should sound like something a real person might say out loud to a reporter.
- If possible, use quotes from people who will validate your findings, add a story, or contribute a practical perspective. You should cultivate these folks before you ask them to give a quote by sending them copies of studies in advance that you'll release publicly. Even if they don't want you to quote them in the press release, you can refer reporters to them for a second perspective.
- Keep it short: short sentences, short paragraphs, and a short article. Aim for 300 words or so. However, many press releases are now longer since they might be published in full in electronic publications.
- To conform to an old custom, add ### to the very end of your press release to signal the end of the story.

Box 6.4. Example of a Press Release for a Journal Article

Support for Medicaid expansion strong among low-income adults

For immediate release: Wednesday, October 8, 2014

Boston, MA—Low-income adults overwhelmingly support Medicaid expansion and think the government-sponsored program offers health care coverage that is comparable to or even better in quality than private health insurance coverage, according to a new study from Harvard School of Public Health (HSPH) researchers. The study appears online October 8, 2014, in *Health Affairs*.

"In the debate over whether or not states should participate in Medicaid expansion, we rarely hear the perspectives of those

Box 6.4. Example of a Press Release for a Journal Article (*cont.*)

people most directly impacted by policies surrounding Medicaid," said study co-author Benjamin Sommers, assistant professor of health policy and economics at HSPH. "Our survey shows that expanding Medicaid under the Affordable Care Act is quite popular among lower-income Americans and that they generally consider Medicaid to be good coverage."

Under the ACA, states can choose whether or not to expand Medicaid to adults with incomes below 138% of the federal poverty level. So far, 27 states and Washington, D.C., are expanding, while 23 states are not—and the issue is controversial in many of the latter states.

Researchers conducted a telephone survey in late 2013 of nearly 3,000 low-income adults in three Southern states—Arkansas, Kentucky, and Texas—that have adopted different approaches to options for Medicaid expansion. . . .

In all three states, nearly 80% of those surveyed said they favored Medicaid expansion, and approximately two-thirds of uninsured adults said they planned to apply for either Medicaid or subsidized private coverage in 2014. . . .

This research was supported by the Commonwealth Fund. . . . Benjamin Sommers was also supported by . . . the Agency for Healthcare Research and Quality (AHRQ).

The study does not reflect the views of the U.S. Department of Health and Human Services.

For more information:
Marge Dwyer
mhdwyer@hsph.harvard.edu
617–432–8416

###

This example has been shortened; the full release is available at http://www.hsph.harvard.edu/news/press-releases/low-income-adults-support-medicaid-expansion/.

Any number of websites will give you examples and further tips on how to write a press release, but these are the key steps. *Inc.* magazine has a particularly good set of hints.[8] Your campus news office might be a good source of models for crafting your own.

You can use a similar format but simpler version for a press advisory. If a current event ties to your work, you can send out an advisory to let the media know you are an available and appropriate expert who would offer some insightful comments on the current issue or event.

The next step is sending out your release or advisory. Work with your news office or your network to identify good targets for faxing or emailing the press releases. Be sure to include any specialty media relevant to your release. Then follow up. The next chapter also shows how to use new social media to get your research into the world.

Talking to Journalists

If you've got your message and talking points clarified for your ideas and research findings, or for a new study that you're releasing, then you're ready to talk to journalists when they call. You know what you want to say, and the next piece is to understand what they're looking for.

One thing they will want is a prompt response when they call or email you. If someone calls about something you're ready to talk about, then call them back right away and do the interview. Journalists are almost always on deadline, and they need a prompt response, even if it's to set up a later time to talk. If you need to collect your thoughts first, ask if you can call back in a few minutes. Or if you have a meeting or class to teach, ask if they can wait for an hour or whatever time you need. Also, you don't have to agree to be interviewed, although you'll want to decline politely, promptly, and helpfully, perhaps suggesting someone better suited to the topic or angle.

Since journalists and the media they work for are a diverse lot, it's impossible to come up with a simple set of rules or specific suggestions for interviews. Some journalists have Ph.D.s; others are just starting out. One journalist might want to know your bottom-line conclusion, and another some of the details about your data or methods. Some might have a strong and informed interest in your field. For example, one *USA Today* reporter I spoke with in the 1990s is now a sociology professor. That's diversity just among *journalists*, and many must meet the needs of diverse media and audiences.

Most journalists are generalists, not specialists in the subject you'll be discussing, though, so my main suggestion is to be prepared to start from scratch with communicating your message, that is, explaining your ideas and findings. At their best, interviews are a conversation between a curious journalist and an interesting and interested source. Here are a few things to keep in mind during that conversation:

- Give the journalist quotes. Even when they are familiar with your topic, they will appreciate clear, simple explanations that they can quote instead of paraphrase, especially on controversial topics.
- Don't make assumptions about what they know or don't know, but also don't talk down to them.
- When you get a call, listen carefully to what the reporter says about the story they're writing and their angle.
- Answer their questions, drawing on your message and talking points.
- You can also ask them questions about what they think or what other sources have told them on the topic.

- If you think they're going in an odd or wrong direction, you can gently suggest an alternative or try to nudge them in a different direction.

Having a conversation also helps you figure out if your message is coming through and the journalist understands your points. Filtering your ideas through another person to get to the public is an act of faith in journalists, to be sure. While that faith is usually well-placed, in my experience, sometimes it's not and you get misquoted or a story gets facts wrong. While misquoting happens, it's annoying but usually fairly benign. Even so, I've known academics who were so afraid of being misquoted that they would not talk to reporters. If control of your message is the most important thing to you, then op-eds, blogs, and radio shows might be better suited to your needs, but you will sacrifice some important opportunities.

One practice that some of my colleagues have tried is to ask if they can see or approve any quotes that the journalist is going to use. However, most journalists won't agree to that because their media outlets have policies to retain editorial control rather than hand it over to sources. Every now and then journalists have asked me to read something that they've written based on our interview, usually to be sure they're correct in their interpretation of a complex idea or fact, not to check a quote.

Radio Shows

Radio is a wonderful genre for talking about research. There are many radio shows across the country, providing lots of opportunities for either short segments on news shows or longer conversations on talk shows. Producers and hosts are always hungry for good content, so include local shows and relevant national shows on your press release list.

Box 6.5. How to Give Great Radio Interviews

Homework before the show:

• Find out about the station, show, and host.

• On call-in shows, find out whether and how callers are screened. You should ask the producer you talk to about this. If there's little screening, or if the show has an audience likely to ask you hostile or difficult questions, do some planning in advance to craft good answers to those tough questions.

• Think about your message before you go on the air. Jot some notes to remind yourself of key points to make. Since no one can see you, you can have your notes in front of you during the interview—but don't read them for your answers.

• Ask your friends or students if you have any speech habits that might be distracting in an interview, like "umms," starting every answer with "Well, . . ." or "So . . . ," or using "sort of" too frequently.

• Prepare and practice answers to some common questions:

   • Tell us about your new book/study/article.

   • Why did you write this book (conduct this study)?

   • Why is this finding surprising?

• Right before the show, warm up your voice a little—chant or sing to relax your vocal chords. Breathe deeply to relax yourself while you're waiting to go on.

During the show:

• Use vivid stories to make your points.

• Listen to the questions carefully and try to answer them, but don't feel bound to the narrow content of the question. Remember your messages and talking points.

• Try to make your remarks conversational.

• Jot down the host's name and the names of other guests on the show, and use their names where appropriate.

• Answer questions in short chunks. Use short sentences and not too many of them.

• Remember to breathe. If you feel out of breath, you're using sentences that are too long.

• Remember to pause to give the interviewer or host time to ask questions. You can't see them, which makes it easy to go on for too long.

• I like to stand up when doing a radio interview.

• Have some water nearby, and know where your mute button is if you have to cough.

If a news show is interested in your work, they will generally call you or email you like any print media reporter would, but they'll ask if you're willing and ready to record an interview over the phone. They might talk to you for five minutes or even longer but use only a short quote or two from you on the air. Some radio shows will patch you in over the phone—use a landline if possible. For longer news segments or for segments that won't be aired right away, you might be asked to go to a nearby studio. I've done lots of interviews from our local NPR affiliate on campus.

Talk shows usually involve more vetting. A producer or other staff member will interview you on the phone, asking about your work and getting a sense of whether you'd make for a good guest on their show. If they are interested, they will either set up a time with you for a phone interview (possibly live) or might book studio space at a local public radio station for you to be interviewed from.

Television Appearances

With many cable channels and a growing number of web-based shows, you're likely to end up on television at some point.[9] Most of the radio basics apply here. But if you've got enough time before you're on, put that iPhone to work and practice on camera. Get someone to ask you questions, and be sure to go over your message and talking points. Then watch yourself and look for ways to improve.

Some things are easier on TV—you can see when the host is about to jump in, and you can smile and communicate non-verbally. Being visible obviously adds a new set of challenges, though. The first thing everyone asks is, "What do I wear?" That's actually relatively easy: Look good but not distracting. According to the pros, the best colors to wear are grays, blues, and browns.

Box 6.6. Making a Strong Impression on Television

Looking like a pro on camera:

• When interviewing in studio, make eye contact with the host and don't look at the camera. If you're interviewing remotely with just a camera, do look at the camera.

• Smile! It will help you to relax and project confidence.

• Refer to the show or the host by name.

• Use natural hand gestures that don't distract.

• Relax, breathe, and ground yourself.

• Don't be distracted by the stage crew.

• Assume that everything is being recorded, so don't make off-the-cuff remarks.

• When the interview is over, sit still until the producer or host tells you that you are done.

Sounding like a pro:

• Speak more slowly than usual.

• Vary your voice and avoid a monotone. Try emphasizing one word or phrase in each sentence.

• Make sure to get out your key messages in your first answer—you may get only one opportunity.

• If you're doing a taped interview and you make a mistake, ask if you can stop and start over.

• If a host asks you a detailed, multipart question, focus on answering the one part that leads you back to your key messages.

Pastels work for shirts or blouses. You don't want to wear white or black, and avoid clothes or neckties with patterns. Makeup is a good idea, since it hides the sweat that's hard to avoid, and usually someone can help you or apply it for you at the studio.

There are basically three options for *how* the interview could happen in a technical sense. If you have a choice, an in-studio interview has many advantages, including the fact that you'll have a better chance to establish a rapport with the host. Satellite and other technologies allow those of us who work outside of big urban areas to be available quickly and cheaply, so see if your university has a television studio for remote interviews. And sometimes a television crew will come to you, especially if your research is in the news. If that happens, be a good host and make it easy for them: Give them directions, arrange for their parking, contact your media office, and help the crew find interesting visuals to use.

Don't forget to use your own social media networks to plug your appearance, both before and after the show, and tag the outlet that you're appearing in.

Op-Eds

Publishing one's opinion on an issue in a newspaper (or magazine) gives an engaged scholar the bully pulpit many of us crave. But getting those 800-or-less words into print requires an understanding of what newspapers are looking for and an ability to write in a different way. Robert Jensen captures the experience many of us have had: "An effective op/ed is not so much a product of writing but of rewriting and editing."[10]

You can find lots of suggestions for writing op-eds. Jensen's book *Writing Dissent* provides lots of examples and suggestions

Box 6.7. Getting Op-Eds Published

How to say it:

• Use a current hook to motivate the piece.

• Get to your point quickly, usually in the first paragraph.

• Make your unique perspective and expertise clear.

• Don't use jargon.

• Don't use footnotes, although op-eds that will be published online might include hypertext links.

• Use short sentences and short paragraphs.

• Use examples or personal stories to illustrate your point.

• Use evidence to support your point.

• Address any common or obvious counterarguments.

• Offer possible solutions to problems you identify. And don't hedge in your recommendations—"President Obama should do xyz" is better than "President Obama could do xyz."

• Mercilessly edit your piece.

How to get it published:

• A few papers will not accept op-eds that are under consideration elsewhere, so you might need to submit the op-ed to one publication at a time.

• Stick to the word limit, usually 750–800 words. Look up and follow the guidelines for the publication outlet you're targeting.

• Have a list of possible outlets in mind.

• Craft a cover letter that explains why your op-ed has an important perspective that is worth publishing.

• Follow-up your email or cover letter with a call to the editor. Write out your carefully crafted pitch to grab the editor's interest.[a]

a Thanks to Stephanie Coontz for the idea to write it out.

for getting even radical ideas into the mainstream. The Op-Ed Project was formed to increase the number of women writers on op-ed pages, and the organization offers seminars on writing op-ed essays and other communication issues (www.theopedproject. org/). Environmentalist Bill McKibben offers some useful tips, too.[11] Finally, read op-eds, both in the big publications and relevant local newspapers, to see what works and to learn from successful writers.

There's no magic formula for getting op-eds published, but persistence is crucial. Most of us who have been successful have a folder full of unpublished pieces for each one that found a home. Teresa Ghilarducci kept sending the *New York Times* op-eds that pointed out big problems with the current pension system, but none got published. Her luck changed the day the New York state legislature cut public employee pensions, and the *Times* asked her to rewrite one she'd already sent them to connect it to the news hook.

But don't wait for the *New York Times* or *Washington Post* to call. Be proactive by writing a piece and getting it published somewhere. Then you can leverage that hit by sending a link out to your network and more broadly through social media. If your ideas are valuable in the larger context of the issue, you can make your op-ed influential no matter where it is published. One op-ed can turn into another, as your experience and reputation snowball. Women's studies professor Allison Piepmeier blogged for publications as varied as the *New York Times* and *skirt! magazine,* and eventually she landed a regular column for the *Charleston City Paper.*

Testimony before Policymakers

Public commissions, legislative bodies, and other public decision-making institutions often invite or allow citizens and recognized experts to offer their knowledge and opinions. When your knowledge is relevant to an issue and an opportunity to testify arises, think about testifying.

First, you need to know who can testify and how to do it. State legislatures and city councils often have open hearing processes, and generally any citizen can arrive early to sign up for a slot to speak to their elected representatives. Your network comes in handy here, so ask your own representative or their staff whether you'd be appropriate and what the requirements are, such as sign-ups, time limits, the possibility of written testimony, or any other rules. When legislators or advocates encourage or invite particular experts to appear, they sometimes find ways to make the process a little less time-consuming—ask about when you're likely to testify. I've sat through hearings in state legislatures that went on for many hours, sometimes late into the night and well past the bedtimes and patience of legislators on the committee, who had gradually disappeared. Congressional hearings require an invitation to appear in person, but usually you can submit written testimony to a committee without an invitation.

Second, the best way to start is to read testimony from earlier hearings on similar issues, which you're likely to find on the committee's or legislature's website. You might find actual testimony on video in the web archives of state legislatures and the U.S. Congress. Based on my own observations and input from colleagues (especially Brad Sears), Box 6.8 provides some tips to start with.

Box 6.8. Testifying as an Expert

What to say:

- Start by acknowledging the chair of the committee and the members, and thank them for the opportunity to testify. Briefly say who you are and your position (i.e., source of expertise).

- Lead with your conclusion and why it's relevant to the policymakers and piece of legislation.

- Give practical conclusions. Be explicit about how your ideas or research are relevant to the problem or bill being considered.

- Don't try to do a comprehensive literature review. If your conclusions are consistent with or different from existing research, you can mention it to add credibility, but only if it's relevant.

- Don't start with theoretical predictions (as you would in an academic paper) and don't use theoretical jargon (or, if jargon is absolutely necessary, explain it). Put any theoretical discussion in practical terms.

How to say it:

- Make eye contact. Be sure to look up at the legislators from time to time. (That can be tricky because they often sit above the witnesses.)

- Don't go over your time limit.

- Practice!

- Memorize your first paragraph so you can look at the committee members in the introductory part of your testimony.

- Ignore the busy-ness of the rest of the room—staffers and legislators will be going in and out of the chamber.

- Practice being respectful but conversational in your tone rather than giving a formal speech. They need your expertise and you're there to explain what you know. They're going to appreciate the time you've taken to do the research and to come testify (they may even make a point of thanking you). One way to think about this is that you're all peers who have a great deal of respect for the process of government in which you're participating and the chamber in which you're sitting.

Conclusion

As you participate within and across these different forums, you will develop your voice and a unique angle that will help to generate additional communication opportunities. Success breeds success—the more you're quoted, the more you'll be sought after to participate in these public spaces.

(Co-authored with Scott Swenson)

Lisa Wade and Gwen Sharp started the Sociological Images blog to encourage people to "develop their sociological imagination." The blog features many kinds of images, from cartoons about academia to charts from studies, but also vintage anti-suffragette postcards, old ads showing gender or racial stereotypes, and photos of Russian greenhouses to illustrate the carbon footprint of roses on Valentine's Day. Their website now gets more than half a million visits per month by readers seeking images and insights gleaned from academic studies and other sources. The blog's posts are cited heavily in the traditional media—newspapers, magazines, radio and TV shows—and in numerous cross-postings on other blogs. One hundred thousand people now follow the blog regularly through Facebook, Twitter, and Pinterest, as well.[1]

In addition to the traditional media and communications options, new social media like the Sociological Images blog provide many more possible routes to engage with various publics, making potentially thousands or even millions of people just a few network links away from our ideas and findings. These twenty-first-century media are now well-known but still relatively novel, especially for those of us who came of scholarly age before their emergence and are struggling to keep up.

Many of us are probably still trying to decide if it's worth investing time in building a social media presence, or whether this is just a passing fad. Over the course of writing this book, Lee has had to confront this very decision—should I tweet?—and ended up enlisting communications expert Scott Swenson to give her a Twitter pep talk and to co-author this chapter.[2] Scott sees social media as a new form of communicating that has changed the landscape forever, not just a passing fancy. In his view, we're talking about a Gutenberg-level innovation, not eight-track tape or the Betamax VCR. If you want to influence policy or media, then go where democracy and debate are most dynamic: social media.

We've found some inspiring examples of academics who use social media very effectively to extend their reach and influence. Raul Pacheco-Vega, an assistant professor of public administration at the Center for Economic Research and Teaching in Mexico, has consciously developed his professional social media presence through a blog, Twitter, and Facebook. His website (www.raulpacheco.org) is a great example of how to use online resources to catalog research, conference presentations, published writing, and tips for professors and students. Pacheco-Vega's blog tagline rather wonkishly defines his field of study as "understanding and solving intractable resource governance problems," but his tweets and blog posts demonstrate a lively interest in water and sanitation policy issues. He has an impressive number of followers—more than 8,000 on Twitter alone. Many of them are also academics, but some are lawyers, activists, journalists, and NGO leaders. Through his social media presence, Pacheco-Vega is defining his niche, developing an audience of people working in the same area, and helping to frame the conversation on these issues. He's also establishing a professional network through his research and his interest in connecting other scholars that has raised his visibility in academia, as well.

Pacheco-Vega is a good example of an assistant professor you may never have heard of, but his social media presence makes it more likely that eventually you will. At the other end of the spectrum are superstar academics who put their reputations on the line using social media to influence public policy in more direct ways.

Most notable among academic social media celebrities is Harvard Law professor Lawrence Lessig. In less than a year, he raised $11 million online from 68,000 people to fund Mayday PAC, a citizen-led "Super PAC to end all Super PACS."[3] In 2014, Mayday PAC used the money it had raised online to support candidates backing reforms that reduce money's influence on democracy. And, yes, Lessig embraces the irony! And no, he didn't win any of his targeted races, but true to his academic character, he "learned important lessons."

How could a university professor raise that kind of money? Lessig is an example of simplicity in social media. He uses the microblogging site Tumblr (lessig.tumblr.com) to keep things easy. He is most active on Twitter (@lessig), though, where he engages a wide range of journalists and legal, public policy, and other experts, as well as ordinary citizens among his 341,000-plus followers. Lessig has combined his reputation as a leading constitutional scholar and his social media savvy to raise awareness of what he sees as the threat posed to our democracy by big money in politics.

Lessig's blog and Twitter presence help frame an emerging public debate, but they are just the most personally visible evidence of his expansion into activism. Before he created Mayday PAC, he first connected with like-minded citizens around the country by working to launch Rootstrikers, a largely social media–driven organization that directs citizens to specific efforts to combat the influence of money in politics.

Lessig's social media celebrity is rare among academics but it need not be. You may not aspire to raise millions online or to become so politically active. Maybe, just as he spotted an issue in his field that needs to be addressed, you see an issue related to your own research that social media can help raise awareness of—but you have to be present on social media first. Don't let one extremely successful example intimidate you. Even Lessig had to figure out the basics of social media, as his current Tumblr tagline indicates: "The slow awakenings of Lessig's once-hibernated blog."

In this chapter, we share thoughts on building a social media presence into your personal communications strategies. This means thinking about which platforms will have the most value in getting your message into the world and in building your network. The main goal, though, is to show you how to get started. It sounds simple to start up a blog or Twitter account, and in some ways it is. Learning the ropes of social media isn't much harder than learning how to work with the electronic tools required by most universities (such as email, websites, and course management software). The hard part comes in thinking about what you want to accomplish, and how to use these media to achieve your goals. How do you get people to pay attention to your blog posts or tweets? How do you get the kind of readership that Wade and Sharp get on Sociological Images? How can you get people to feature your research or retweet your tweets, as Lessig does? We will help you be strategic to get the most out of the social media world.

Why Build a Social Media Presence?

The numbers alone make a convincing case for incorporating social media into your own communications work. Facebook launched in 2004 and has more than a billion users, and Twitter came along two years later and boasts over a quarter billion users.[4] Add to those media the opportunities to have a channel on You-Tube, build a personal website, or cultivate a devoted readership on your blog, and you've got a do-it-yourself communications plan that can reach deeply into the world you want to influence.

Although the vast numbers of social media users might be enough to convince some to get onboard, we know lots of skeptics who have doubts: Isn't this shameless self-promotion? Who has time to blog or tweet? Does anybody who matters read that stuff?

Like other communications strategies discussed in this book, there is an element of promotion involved, and social media are potentially powerful tools. Develop some effective materials that describe your study (including a message and talking points), then get the word out and be prepared to engage with people who respond to your work. So in addition to the distribution of a press release and other connections with traditional media, you would also use all of the social media that you are engaged in to spread the word about new research findings, for example. Post the study itself online, so that you've got a more substantive place to point readers.[5] Then you can use a short post on Facebook (a status update), send out a series of tweets, and use available blog opportunities to release an artfully worded, very short summary and link. Ask your friends to repost or retweet. If you get press coverage, that's another opportunity to post something. If you can come up with a graphic way to represent your findings, share that, too.

People in those spaces will respond—that's what engagement is all about.

However, understanding the larger value of social media requires a shift away from seeing it just as a high tech way to send out a self-serving press release farther and wider. This book's basic message about how to become an effective engaged public professor, pra-cademic, public intellectual, or scholar-activist—or whatever you might call yourself—is about finding a useful role in the larger pub-lic conversation or debate about important public concerns. Social media give academics the opportunity to show themselves as real human beings engaged in a broad conversation, not just as self-promoting wonks. People who use it only for self-promotion are missing the boat. Think beyond your individual work to the broader field, like a good editor or producer would in publishing or broad-casting, and provide good content, original or not, to help set the terms of debate for your issue or field. If you want a reputation as having a command of the issues and as someone people will want to network with, you need to get out of just a "me" perspective and into "we." Social media are about being social, transparent, and connected. Build a following, and trust that the people who need to see your tweets or blog posts will find you.

Getting Started

You've got lots of options among social media platforms and strat-egies, and new ones pop up on a regular basis. The possibilities might seem bewildering, so we recommend focusing on a few with particular relevance and value right now for scholars and researchers: some basic blogging (most likely as a guest blogger), and developing a presence on Facebook, Twitter, and LinkedIn. Each of the big platforms involves some start-up investment of time to learn about how it works and to build a following, but once established, the maintenance time on social media can be very manageable. Start-up and maintenance time for blogging is much more variable, depending on whether you have your own blog or are a guest blogger.

These new social media evolve rapidly and can be intimidating to rookies. If you're completely new, start simply and don't hesitate to ask for help. Your graduate assistants or undergraduate students can probably teach you a thing or two in reciprocation for all you are teaching them. But don't just task them with doing it. Take time to learn from them, as you will want to understand how to explore and connect with colleagues, media, and others interested in the issues you care about. An investment in learning more about social media can pay off in big ways. And building a following in one space will help with developing a presence in another.

Facebook

Obviously, if a billion people are already on Facebook, including 57% of Americans,[6] most readers of this book probably are, too. In posting pictures of our vacations, gardens, or kids, many of us think of this space as a way to keep up with friends, family, and other acquaintances (and, if you're like us, a fair number of people you've never even met). We completely shed our professional personas in those spaces at some risk, though, since it's hard to keep Facebook posts private. Ill-chosen words about an issue or person could come back to haunt us at some point. If you're venturing into public engagement, develop an awareness about how your Facebook posts might be perceived in the contexts you work in. At a minimum, you don't want to undermine your work in those contexts with your Facebook persona.

Beyond that minimum, Facebook presents an enormous, positive opportunity to connect your work with the general public, and it's easy to get started (see Box 7.1). Many adult users go to Facebook to learn about the news and how to help others.[7] Share a link to something you've written or post an insightful comment about an issue and it will go to your friends. Then the power of the network takes over to extend that message. If you are a typical Facebook user, you've got about 200 friends (the median number of friends for adults, so half have more, and half have less), and your friends have about 200 friends each. Potentially, then, your post could reach 40,000 people in just one round of sharing. A second round would boost that exponentially to a potential 8 million people (200 times 40,000). That won't happen, of course, since it assumes no overlap in your networks and a 100% sharing rate, both unrealistic assumptions. But it doesn't take a high sharing rate to get your post to thousands or more people quickly. Even a tiny fraction would get your short post out to many more people than an academic journal article would reach.

These numbers show why people who want to get attention for something they care about are on Facebook. With some knowledge and practice, you can improve your chances of someone sharing your posts. Once you've made that investment in understanding how it works, your time requirements can be pretty short. Box 7.1 tells you how to get started on Facebook. Some tips for successful Facebook and Twitter posts are in Box 7.4.

Twitter

The number one reason to be on Twitter? That's where the journalists are—all day, everyday—talking to each other. An academic doesn't need thousands of followers to succeed in social media.

Box 7.1. Getting Started with Facebook

Sign up: Go to facebook.com and sign up. You don't need any-thing in particular. Be sure to look at the section on privacy prefer-ences to choose who gets to see the stuff you post.

Find some friends: "Friend" is a verb on Facebook—this requires a little time. You can search for people you know with the search tool, or import contacts from Google or other lists that Facebook sees. Think broadly about friends, and include the people in your network—elected officials love Facebook. Send a friend request, and accept requests from people who send them to you. Look at your friends' friends and friend them, too.

Post something in your Update Status box: You become part of the big distribution network, and your Facebook friends will start to see you as someone with something to say.

Like and share other people's posts: When you see other people's posts that fit into the type of content that you are posting, "share" it with your friends, too. Facebook culture is a sharing culture, and reciprocity rules.

Experts will draw people of like mind in the field, and the people covering that field.

Twitter is different from Facebook in many ways, the most significant of which is the brevity of thought forced by the 140-character (not word) limit. For many academics, the idea of saying anything in so few words seems impossible until they see it done well and then jump into the conversation! If brevity is the soul of wit, Twitter is the body that encompasses that soul.

Another major difference is structure. Facebook is a microblog-ging site for short-form posts that people either "like" or share or comment on. It's more static, drawing on connections that already exist.

By contrast, Twitter is a conversation in the global public square, all day, every day. People who "follow" you on Twitter want to see your posts, which land in their Twitter feed. You can also connect with total strangers through the use of hashtags (they look like this: #wordswithnospace), classifying tweets based on user interest. By using hashtags, people have real-time conversations during live events, TV programs, elections, and even academic conferences. Raul Pacheco-Vega has created new hashtags to enhance community building among scholars: #ScholarSunday is for passing along Twitter handles (or usernames) of academics worth following, and #MyResearch is for scholars to use to publicize their own research findings.[8] Hashtags are also often used for humor, irony, or sarcasm, as in #duh.

Perhaps the best description contrasting Twitter and Facebook we've heard is this: Facebook is for people you went to high school with. Twitter is for people you wish you went to high school with. It's all about chosen community, shared interests, or public debate with people with different perspectives.

A common refrain after people first glance at Twitter is, "I can't do that. I'm busy. Who has time to waste like that?" It is overwhelming, so start small. Start with a short period of observing Twitter to sort out the people, organizations, and resources that you want to follow. If you're thinking about how to use Twitter professionally, you could begin your explorations through a hobby, sport, play, TV show, or musician you like. Using Twitter's search function, identify the hashtags associated with that personal interest of yours, and read through the conversations to see who is engaged and what they're talking about. In other words, make it fun first, so that when it becomes work, you'll approach that with an understanding of how to make it more enjoyable.

Other than using hashtags to find people talking about the things you are interested in, another way to find community on Twitter is to engage others directly. You do that by retweeting

Box 7.2. Getting Started with Twitter

Sign up: Go to twitter.com and sign up for an account. You'll need to create a username, or "handle." Settings allow you to send every tweet to your Facebook page, too.

Bio: Your Twitter bio is your calling card for visitors. In your observational period, look at people you know or admire on Twitter and see how they use their bio space. Pay attention to the type of photo they use as well as the background images in their headers and elsewhere on their page. Every piece conveys something about you and helps people see you as you want to be seen in the world, or at least on Twitter.

Find some hashtags for conversations you want to be part of: Make a list of hashtags that the people you follow use. Search for those hashtags and see the conversations that are happening. Use Twitter's search box to find the hashtags that relate to your research. Use them in your tweets.

Follow other people: Find and follow people you know or admire in your areas of research or discipline. You will see their tweets on your Twitter feed (also known as your home timeline) when you sign into Twitter. Look at the people they follow.

Develop followers: One way to get followers is to follow others, a rough norm of reciprocity. Include your Twitter handle in your email address, business card, and web bios. Ask your friends and colleagues to follow you—and make it worth their while with good tweets.

Tweet: The 140-character limit is strict, and it takes some time before it feels (somewhat) natural. Truth is, it's actually best to keep your tweets to 120 characters or less, because you want people to retweet you—when they do, your Twitter handle is included, making the tweet longer. Give it a try. Take advantage of opportunities to tweet a comment on a news story or recent research, possibly your own. You can also tweet a "thanks" to any reporter who cites your work, fostering an ongoing relationship with journalists who have an interest in what you have to say. Once you feel more comfortable, live tweet an event that might be of interest to your followers.

And retweet: Retweeting helps the people you follow and your followers to spread their messages. Retweet posts that you like, and use your retweets to build a community. Retweeting journalists' tweets is a way to say thank you and to give their work, and maybe yours, more exposure. If there's space, you can add your own message if you want to.

Mention people in your tweets: If you put a user's Twitter handle into your message, it will also go to them as a "mention."

(RT) people's tweets you like. If their tweets are too long (Twitter adds their @name when you retweet, making it a little longer), then you can modify their tweet (MT) by shortening some of their phrasing. Adding an MT at the front of a post indicates to people that you've modified the original.

You can also reply to someone to engage in conversation. When you do that, their @name will appear at the front of your tweet back to them. In addition to the person you're replying to, your reply shows up on the Twitter feed of anyone who follows *both* of you. So if Lee replies to Scott's tweet, we would each see the reply, and the three people who follow both of us would see it in their feed, too. And here's a potentially helpful, little-known trick: If you want your followers and theirs to see your reply, too, add a period before it, .@name. That makes your reply viewable to others, not just to the person to whom you are replying and anyone who happens to follow both of you, so Lee's reply would go to all of her followers and to all of Scott's. To be clear, no reply is ever private as it always appears in your timeline and theirs—it's just a matter of whether your followers and theirs see it too. The only way to say something private on Twitter is to direct message (DM) a person and you can do that only if they follow you, too.

People want to connect—that's why social media are ultimately successful. Raul Pacheco-Vega makes his social media presence obvious so readers can easily connect with him. He uses a limited number of tags to classify his posts, making it easy to find his thoughts on different topics. His writing style is friendly, providing information that is useful to his audience, and not always about research, but often about the "how to" aspect of being an academic.

Box 7.3. Everybody Starts at the Beginning with Social Media

Scott Swenson's story: Despite years in the communications business, I was slow to get involved with Twitter, Facebook, and blogs. Then in 2006 someone decided that, even though I had no expertise in social media, I should be hired to create a blog on one of the most controversial public policy issues of our time: reproductive health. The site, RH Reality Check, allowed me to learn social media on the job—and very publicly, in front of a niche and highly critical audience of experts. Many in our audience had their own blogs, organizational or otherwise, and we were all competing for attention. And those were just my political allies.

Eventually, I started a personal blog, but later abandoned it. I decided that Facebook was my blog, given the lack of time I have for writing now. The newsy things I want to comment on I do on Facebook and Twitter, with enough space to add 50–200 of my own words if I'm so moved. For me, the first rule of Twitter (and social media more generally) is to make it fun before you make it work. Remove the anxiety of "getting it right" and replace that with simple joy as the best path to learning something new.

Now, social media is where I live. I get most of my news from a much wider variety of sources thanks to the people I follow and friend on social media. I'm in touch with colleagues and friends from every part of my life, and we're building deeper friendships with new people because we share and know more about our work and our lives beyond work. My advice: Emphasize the social, share yourself, engage with cranky uncles, and use your free speech to inform and educate. Know that your greatest ability to influence the world begins with those closest to you and ripples out from there to become, potentially, tidal waves of change.

The importance of connecting brings us back to a version of our initial question—why Twitter? As with everything else in social media, it's because that's where the conversation is today and will be for the foreseeable future. Compared with Facebook, Twitter is also the social media location for a slightly more elite audience of people who want to know news first: journalists and public policy makers. If you see reporters or others on Twitter talking about your field, you can insert your expertise by offering a simple stat or fact either from your own research or from studies you know, and then you've started to build a reputation as someone with useful information. Conrad Hackett, a demographer at the Pew Research Center, has journalists from around the world among his 109,000 followers who value his vivid tweets of images from many sources. His visuals include things like simple tables showing who believes in evolution (67% of Democrats, but only 43% of Republicans), graphs tracing trust in government (a long, mostly downward trend since 1960), and a map showing the countries that have been invaded by England at some point in history (nine out of ten). If you watch the trending topics bar in the left column of your homepage, you might also be able to insert your research or ideas into a conversation that is, at that moment, very popular on Twitter.

Twitter commentary can even help shape the news. Black Twitter—the collective Twitter voice of African Americans, particularly of young black women, who are disproportionately on the platform—created powerful hashtags like #BlackLivesMatter and #ICantBreathe. Activists like Alicia Garza, Johnetta Elzie, and DeRay Mckesson created those hashtags and live-tweeted protests.[9] Their efforts on Twitter contributed to the national outcry and mobilized protesters after the acquittal of George Zimmerman in the Trayvon Martin shooting and after the nonindictments in Ferguson and Staten Island.[10]

On a lighter note, in 2013 economist Justin Wolfers was looking for something interesting to tweet about in a boring report on inflation from the Bureau of Labor Statistics.[11] Digging deeper, he found a tasty tidbit that he tweeted to his 76,000 followers, along with a graph of price changes over the preceding decade:

> We have entered CUPCAKE DEFLATION. The price index for "Fresh cakes and cupcakes" fell -0.8% over the past year.[12]

While you might think that's a tweet only an economist could love, over the next couple of days CNNMoney, *Marketplace*, MarketWatch, and Australian Business Review all covered the story, and you can follow the ongoing conversation at #cupcakedeflation.

Look for those opportunities to join or start a conversation and add value to it in productive ways. You'll be able to spot the self-promoters easily. Study them, then do the opposite. Like life, be the kind of friend you want in others. Kindness and humility in social media go a long way toward establishing your presence. So speak when spoken to, thank people for RTs and MTs, and be respectful when engaging others (especially those you disagree with). Studies show that people who are polite and ask others to "please RT" actually have higher RT rates.[13] Over time and with consistency you'll become a trusted resource on Twitter and will perhaps be asked for a quote or interview, or to give a talk or contribute a paper or chapter to a project in your field. At least part of your community, no matter what it is, is on Twitter. Find your tribe, or beat your own drum and they will come.

Box 7.4. A Few Other Elements of Good Social Media Posts

Grab readers' attention: For blog posts, craft engaging titles. Put keywords in the first sentence to make it easy for readers to know what you're writing about. Twitter posts are an art form, since 140 characters doesn't give you a lot of space to make a unique and engaging point. Over time, you will probably develop your own style.

Use images: Justin Wolfers and Conrad Hackett show how valuable images can be in making a point. On Facebook, images and photos guarantee more attention. Twitter is catching up with more visual sites and has made sharing photos and videos much easier. When you have only 140 characters, the thousand words a picture paints come in handy. Charts, images, video, or other graphic elements that help bring your research to life are as important on Twitter as anywhere.

Time your posts and tweets: Free blogging software like Hootsuite, TweetDeck, or Buffer will allow you to time your posts so you can maintain a social media presence while you're in class or meetings, or even while you sleep. Those sites will help you schedule your tweets, just in case you don't want to spend all day on Twitter. You can spend a few minutes each day planning and scheduling tweets to appear at different times so that you maintain your online presence. These apps also shorten links for you in order to save characters in your tweets. With these apps on your smartphone, you can quickly check in and respond to whatever's going on when you have a few extra minutes in your day, on public transportation, a lunch break, or between classes.

Interact: If people comment on your post, say something back.

Box 7.5. Sample Tweets

Zerlina Maxwell (@ZerlinaMaxwell):
> Don't tell me I need a gun. Or a taser. Or a whistle. Or special nail polish. Teach men not to rape. #rapecultureiswhen

> I don't want to live in the Wild Wild West. I shouldn't need a gun on every first date to be safe from assault. #rapecultureiswhen

Raul Pacheco-Vega (@raulpacheco):
> Water cooperation does not always equal greater regional stability—@paulahanasz #ISA2015 #TA79 causes of water conflict not addressed

> If we (as academics) are supposed to bridge the divide with policy makers we need ways to spread our research broadly (SocMed) #ISA2015

Arindrajit Dube (@arindube):
> Will Wal-Mart's wage hike cause firms competing for minimum wage workers (e.g. fast food) to also raise wages? #monopsony #spillover

Stephen Russell (@StephnTRussell):
> In spite of bullying, LGBT kids who come out in high school have more life satisfaction. @heidistevesn13

Mark Hugo Lopez (@mhugolopez):
> Today was the day that 300k unauthorized immigrants who came to US as kids could have applied for deportation relief

Blogging

Blogging is an outlet that, at least in theory, can reach anyone in the world with access to a web browser. In addition to potentially unlimited access to an audience, there are no gatekeepers and no word limits as in microblogging. Not surprisingly, it's become a tempting outlet for scholars who want a larger audience. For a lot of academics, blogging seems to be synonymous with engagement.

Should you blog? Our advice is to think it through carefully. We've seen several friends with great ideas and good intentions start up blogs that they later abandoned, as did Scott with his personal blog. The time they had to spend did not seem worth whatever value they thought blogging provided. The trade-off is clear: time for blogging and marketing the blog vs. time for research and other engagement projects. You want to make sure the value of the blog is sufficient to justify the time—that's the key consideration in making your decision.

First, what will your blog add to the conversation? Political scientist John Sides, founder of the Monkey Cage blog, advises his fellow political scientists to "choose topics to which you can add value as a political scientist."[14] His intention with his own blog is to summarize research in his field for a broader audience and then to use that research to reflect on current events.

Second, what will *you* get out of it for the time you put in? Bloggers like Sides and Sociological Images' Wade have noted several valuable outcomes:

- Blogs provide content for courses.
- A successful and engaging blog can make you an expert sought out by others. For example, Wade has been approached by the *New York Times, Wall Street Journal*, NPR, and television shows to comment on

gender and culture issues, like the appropriateness of sexy Halloween costumes for girls and other products marketed to girls and women.

- Blogs push academics to become generalists, which can come in handy for teaching courses that stretch outside our areas of specialization.
- Blogging can also be a research tool. Sides argues for using a blog as "a long-running test-drive of a research project," strengthening a writing practice, and generating reactions from readers that can improve your ideas.[15]
- Blogging on disciplinary research is not only a service to your profession, but it helps to build what Sides calls "appreciative thinking" skills.[16] Being able to see the positive value of research pushes us past the purely critical inclinations that we often have.
- Blogging can be fun.

You could add to the list the fact that prestigious news outlets sometimes buy up blogs, enriching their founders. The *New York Times* acquired Nate Silver's FiveThirtyEight, which later moved to ESPN. The *Washington Post* acquired and now publishes the Monkey Cage blog.

Third, will your blog get the audience you want? Amitai Etzioni puts it succinctly: "Given that the whole purpose of the public intellectual is not just to speak, but also to be heard, it is important to note that blogging often will not get you much of a hearing."[17] Getting attention for your blog is the big challenge in an increasingly crowded online marketplace of ideas. Marketing a blog also adds to the time you'll need to spend, although you can choose how broadly you want to aim and adjust your time commitment accordingly.

Etzioni's advice is to connect with blogs that have an established readership. A recent month of his own blog (www.amitai-etzioni.org/) shows how to do that. Every post was "cross-posted" from somewhere else, including the Huffington Post, CNN, *Dissent*, *The National Interest*, and *Boston Review*. Etzioni's posts did double duty for him, providing content for his own blog, which has become a kind of library of his blog posts, and connecting to additional audiences for his ideas.

If you decide that creating your own blog is a worthwhile project, then go into it ready to invest some time, and use that time wisely. Box 7.6 gives you some tips from Wade, Sides, and others for writing effective blog posts. Box 7.7 provides some ideas from the same folks for expanding your reach.

You don't have to have your own blog to be part of the blogosphere, though. If you decide that creating a blog is not for you right now, you can still participate by commenting on blog posts, communicating with bloggers, and guest blogging. In fact, we would go so far as to recommend guest blogging as the preferred

Box 7.6. Tips for Good Blogging

- Write short posts and get to the point quickly.
- Create a distinctive tone for your posts.
- Take a unique or counterintuitive perspective.
- Practice and be patient—you'll get better.
- You don't have to be a specialist to post on a topic.
- Carefully choose titles of blog posts and the first sentence of posts—that can change the likelihood that your post will come up in searches.
- Tags are like keywords that capture the topic areas of your post. They allow people to search for a topic easily, so choose them wisely.
- Summarize research and make it accessible to a lay audience. (Sides)
- Recruit other authors for your blog. (Sides)
- Post timely material and update your blog a lot.

Box 7.7. Tips for Marketing

- Cross-post on other blogs that are more widely read by approaching the editors of those sites and pitching them.
- Use your Facebook, Twitter, Tumblr, and other accounts to post links to your blog.
- Cross-post your blog on sites like Daily Kos (diaries), Reddit, and StumbleUpon (these communities require active involvement to be successful), as well as other sites that allow you to post directly.
- Mobilize your network to drive readers to your blog.
- Take extreme positions to get attention.
- Use short, clever, or even absurd titles.
- If there are other blogs run by academics, journalists, or policymakers holding opposing or different views, disagree with them, linking from your blog to theirs and creating the opportunity for a blog debate. This puts you on the radar of established bloggers writing in the field, and a high-quality and entertaining exchange creates a reason for people to pay attention, comment, and come back. You can also link back to bloggers you agree with, but the opportunity for tension is obviously much less in such cases.
- Use auxiliary sites (e.g., Twitter, Facebook, and Pinterest) to promote your blog.
- The more you post, the more people will link to your blog; more links might even push your blog up on Google searches, although Google's search algorithms are not transparent and unchanging.

route for most academics, unless your particular field has no strong blogger in it. The trade-off is that having your own blog gives more practice in writing in a blog style as opposed to an academic style, and that you have the opportunity to shape the dialog in your field by building a volume of work over time. But the upside of affiliating with or guesting on other blogs is that you can take advantage of their established audiences and the marketing they've done and potentially will do for your piece. The other downside is that like with any other publication, if you want to guest blog, you have to pitch your angle to the blog editor, and some more popular blogs can be hard to get into.

Whether you're a guest blogger or develop your own blog, you will be out in the social media world, open to public reactions and responses. The blogosphere has insightful commentary and interesting debates to take part in, and you can carry on substantive public debates in real time, not academic publishing time. You'll even have the opportunity to have conversations with your audience. (The blogging experience has a negative side, too, which chapter 8 discusses.)

LinkedIn

For the pure professional in you, LinkedIn has evolved from the "post your resume" image it once had into an increasingly social platform. In addition to being a way to systematize your network, LinkedIn now includes status updates and ways to "endorse" the people you're networked with. Those features provide easier interactivity and reasons to come back to the site and see what people are talking about there.

As a way to keep track of your network, LinkedIn is invaluable. By listing publications on the site you call attention to your writing and ideas. Status updates allow you to promote your blog posts and media coverage about your research to your professional networks. LinkedIn is also a great way of keeping in touch with the professionals you help create, your students. Watching their careers is reason enough to establish and maintain a presence on the platform.

A few simple steps can help you keep connected with LinkedIn. People will invite you to connect and might send messages to you.

Deciding whether you will accept an invitation to link or not is a personal choice. Scott accepts all invitations, while Lee accepts only those from people she has actually met.

Other Social Media to Note

YouTube: Producing video content has become relatively easy. Doing it well is another story (see TED Talks). If your content lends itself to a short presentation that is visual, and if you can creatively convey important findings, then you might consider enlisting someone with basic production skills, equipment, and software to produce a short video (three to five minutes) that highlights the story your data tells. Your journalism or communications department or campus audio/visual labs are good resources to start with. Visual content is easily embedded in blog posts and adds an impact that brings your data to life for readers and viewers. Creating a series of short videos might warrant establishing your own YouTube channel to catalog them, another way to reach new audiences for your ideas.

Tumblr: Tumblr is a microblogging platform with an emphasis on visual content. Many users post photos and videos while others use it just for short-form writing, much as Lawrence Lessig does. If you don't have a blog and are thinking of starting one, and you don't want to take the time to master Squarespace, WordPress, or any of the other platforms that allow complete control over the design of your blog, then Tumblr is a good option. Tumblr has its own templates and basic platforms already in place, and it currently hosts nearly 200 million blogs. Its unique feature is that it's a "stumble blog" that allows users to see new blogs of interest as you "tumble" through the site. You can follow and track your favorites, and it's a great way to expose yourself to the array of creative expression in the world.

Pinterest: If you understand community bulletin boards, you understand Pinterest. Users "pin" visual content they find interesting from around the web, sharing all manner of information that can be initially conveyed visually. Have a great recipe (or looking for one)? Pin a photo of the meal with the recipe for others to find. Is there one chart that tells the story of your latest research? Pin it with a short summary and link back to your research.

Google+: Promoted as the second-largest social network after Facebook, Google+ proves that it understands the art of overstatement. According to the *New York Times*, only about half of the 540 million users Google+ claims—including those technically employing Google+ "enhanced properties," such as YouTube commenters—actually use the site monthly.[18] That's still a lot of people, but when you get away from the stats and actually experience how your friends use Google+, what you'll find is they are mostly on other platforms. There may be reasons to invest time in Google+ in the future, but for people just starting out in social media, this is one to put on the bottom of your to do list, at least for now.

Keeping Up and Keeping an Eye Out for New Social Media

Pay attention to the emergence of new options. If you're noticing a trend in the descriptions of the newer social media platforms toward visual content, then you understand that increasingly affordable and accessible technology is giving more people the ability to show as much as they tell. The people who will engage with the public effectively to shape the ideas of the future will be those who understand this and can tap into the visual and audio capabilities that social media bring to our computers, phones, tablets, and televisions.

Again, your students might be the best way to keep up with where social media are going. We have noticed a dynamic in which a popular platform starts feeling too crowded for some audiences. Deciding whether you should follow the early adopters into a new space probably depends on where the people you most want to connect with are going.

The investment in these new social media can pay off big time in growing the audience you want to influence. Political scientist Larry Sabato tweets political commentary and political trivia to 80,000 followers. As a law student, Zerlina Maxwell burst into Twitter fame on election issues and she now tweets on domestic violence, sexual assault, and other race and gender issues to 48,000-plus followers, alongside her fans on satellite radio, cable television, and other media. Both ended up on *Time*'s list of 140 Best Twitter Feeds of 2014.

Channel your inner social media diva to engage with people around the world in real time. Experiment! You can take your time getting into the various social media platforms, and maybe set some limits in terms of the time you spend on any one of them. See which ones work best for you, and then incorporate them into your own communications plan.

8

In the Heat of the Moment

· · · · · · · · · · · · · · · · ·

Managing Public Conflict

The Obama administration hired health economist Jonathan Gruber as a consultant during the design of the Affordable Care Act, also known as Obamacare. Gruber's contribution was a very useful computer model to estimate the budget impact of different versions of health care reforms. He was also known to journalists as being a good explainer of details of the legislation without a lot of jargon, so he was often publicly linked with Obamacare.[1] As some colleagues later reported, though, Gruber's proficiency in explaining economics and health policy vastly exceeded his political savvy.[2]

And that's putting it mildly. In late 2014, the media and opponents of Obamacare discovered videos of Gruber criticizing the reforms that he had helped to create. In one video, Gruber pointed to what he saw as a lack of transparency during the debate over the act that obscured some of its key features, like the tax penalty for not purchasing mandatory insurance and how proponents avoided calling it a "tax." Worse yet, Gruber implied that the lack of transparency, along with "the stupidity of American voters," was essential to getting the ACA passed.

Regardless of whether Gruber was right about a lack of transparency—and plenty of people disagreed with him on that point—his comments were politically ill-advised. Republicans in the House of Representatives hauled him before a committee to explain himself. Over the course of a four-hour hearing, Gruber repeatedly apologized as both Democratic and Republican representatives raked him (the Democrats) and Obamacare (the Republicans) over the coals.[3] The embarrassing spectacle was widely covered on news channels across the political spectrum.

If you're working on a public and highly controversial issue, could you end up in the middle of a big, heated, and visible public debate like Jon Gruber? The odds are good that you won't. Most engagement happens at a level that stays out of the newspapers and at a much lower level of emotional and rhetorical heat.

And yet you've probably heard at least one "horror story" that might give you pause, whether that of Jonathan Gruber or one of the scholars discussed in Box 8.1. Before digging into how to deal with conflict, I think it's important to point out that these events did not lead all of the scholars in question to retreat to their offices and academic audiences, and you shouldn't either.

Doing good research with professional integrity is the best strategy for surviving conflicts over your research, but that isn't sufficient in some situations. The key is to also do a bit of planning if you're in a situation that might someday put you and your work in an uncomfortable spotlight.

Some situations are more likely to get you there than others. If your research hits a cultural or political hot button, like today's heated debates over teen sexuality, climate change, gun control, the minimum wage, charter schools, gay marriage, or evolution, you might attract attention from many people outside of academia who think they have some stake in your research findings or ideas. Or if you become an expert witness in litigation, you could get a

---

Box 8.1. Researchers as Subjects of Controversy

- In 2005, a team of geoscientists (Michael Mann, Ray Bradley, and Malcolm Hughes) received a hostile letter from a powerful congressional committee chairperson demanding detailed information about how their study that provided strong evidence of global warming was funded, the methods they used, and the data they produced.

- Someone illegally hacked into the email messages of another climate scientist, Phil Jones, and made those messages public, leading to accusations and investigations of potential scientific wrongdoing against several scientists (all of which eventually resulted in findings of *no* wrongdoing).

- An advocacy group sent a Freedom of Information Act request to a University of Wisconsin historian, William Cronon, seeking copies of his university email account messages that related to a political debate about collective bargaining rights for public employees.

---

subpoena to produce drafts and other materials that you used to formulate your professional opinion on a topic. Likewise, if you are a professor (especially at a public university) and become visible in a heated political debate, whether it's related to your research or not, you might find yourself the target of an advocacy group's unwanted attention. Even working with smaller local organizations or issues can generate conflict with powerful opponents, although usually not of the headline-grabbing sort.

If you suspect you might someday end up in such a situation, prepare now so that you're ready later: Learn to manage conflict. See what's behind the conflict—often it's politics, not science. Prepare yourself psychologically for the possibility of conflict. And live an ethical professional life.

Avoiding Is Not Managing

One instinctive response might be to just avoid conflict by staying out of the debate. Economist David Card's research has been very influential in changing views on a longstanding debate about the minimum wage. He and his co-author showed that increasing the minimum wage does not necessarily reduce employment, and they argued that there are good theoretical reasons for that finding.[4] Card said his interest in the response to the minimum wage was theoretical, not political: "I try to stay out of political arguments."[5]

In a media interview, Card reported he no longer studies the minimum wage, at least in part because of the controversy that greeted his research: "First, it cost me a lot of friends. People that I had known for many years, for instance, some of the ones I met at my first job at the University of Chicago, became very angry or disappointed. They thought that in publishing our work we were being traitors to the cause of economics as a whole."[6] Card's work upset not only some powerful people in his discipline, but also business interests, generating numerous attacks on his research.

He clearly hoped to avoid those consequences by stepping away from the topic. But the avoidance strategy he implicitly advocated is not foolproof. His—and your—research could still attract controversy, perhaps as a result of attention from other academics or from advocacy efforts. If that happens, being cloistered in your university office will deprive you of some important resources that you would otherwise have had to draw on. In particular, a well-developed professional network includes people who can come to your defense or help you sidestep or mitigate the conflict in the first place.

Staying out of the public eye doesn't mean your research won't be affected by politics, either. In some fields this might not be surprising. In the United States, political pressure has influenced the availability of funding for studies on the effectiveness of gun control policies and related topics. In the mid-1990s, the National Rifle Association was involved in a successful effort to cut funding to the Centers for Disease Control (CDC) that could have been used to study gun control. After that traumatic experience, the CDC has shied away from funding studies that get too close to findings that might rile the industry, according to observers, with the unfortunate secondary impact of reducing the number of people studying firearms.[7] Scholars' involvement in that debate over funding might not have tipped the balance, but avoidance certainly did not shelter researchers from the pain of political barriers to further research.

In my view, a healthier strategy than trying to avoid conflict is managing conflict, both as you plan for it and as you live through it. For some people, managing conflict is really about managing fears: I'll look stupid. My colleagues will lose respect for me. I'll have to spend too much time responding. I might not be as persuasive as those criticizing my work. I might have made a mistake.

Those reactions are perfectly normal, but the scenarios they anticipate aren't that different from the kind of experiences we might have in our scholarly communities, where we sometimes disagree with our students, advisors, colleagues, journal editors, reviewers, or funding agencies. The stakes are different in the public arena—higher, I would argue—and that's what makes us especially nervous.

When Conflict Is about Politics, Not Science

It's all too easy to take criticism or conflict personally and to charge into the public arena to use our academic debating skills.

We're very invested in our own ideas and are ready to defend them in disagreements with other scholars. We're comfortable and proficient within the rules of the academic game, but we have to be aware that the playing field—really, the whole game—shifts dramatically once we're in public engagement mode.

The players in the public game will have varying *interests in* and different *perspectives on* the ideas of scholars. Not surprisingly, a lot of interesting thinkers in the world are not academics but people who have their own theories and data about how the world works, and they draw conclusions based on those perspectives. You will find people like that everywhere, including elected officials, journalists, the clergy, and your next-door neighbor, not to mention the many people who read newspapers and blogs or who come to public talks. Discussions and debates with those folks are one of the joys of public engagement, in my opinion, and they aren't so different from our detailed debates with close academic colleagues.

Some other participants in a given debate might be less pure minded, though, acting more out of a personal, political, or financial interest in the particular findings of research than in the process of uncovering knowledge that might rationally inform public decisions. While those participants might speak the language of science (and might even be scientists), their criticisms of research are likely to be targeted at findings that pose challenges for the pursuit of their own self-interests, or the interests of particular groups. Those are the people to watch out for, and they can be found everywhere.

Naomi Oreskes and Erik Conway are historians of science who have studied public controversies about scientific research that informs public policy. When they analyzed the debates over global warming, acid rain, nuclear arms policy, dangers of smoking, and second-hand tobacco smoke, Oreskes and Conway found the same scientific messengers and same scientific-sounding messages popping up over and over again. Those messengers push back hard against an emerging consensus among scientists in the field—that the earth is warming, cigarettes are bad for your health, we can't "win" a nuclear war, etc.

While those science critics aren't scholars in the fields of research that they are critiquing, they are very influential engaged scholars, using some of the tactics discussed in this book. They deploy their scientific credentials and cultivate political networks, including think tanks and influential political figures with an interest in a free market ideology, to cast doubt on the findings in question.

Oreskes and Conway call those critics "merchants of doubt," since they skillfully exploit the uncertainty built into statistical analyses and the caution that motivates scientific progress. The critics turn uncertainty and caution into doubt about the trustworthiness of the mainstream scientific findings: "They understood the power of language: you could undermine opponents' claims by insisting that theirs were uncertain, while presenting your own as if they were not."[8] Those doubts, in turn, allow the critics to claim that our knowledge isn't sufficient to take policy action on these issues. Policy inaction is in fact usually their goal, according to Oreskes and Conway, allowing the fossil fuel, tobacco, and defense industries that support the critics to continue to profit handsomely.

While these critics of science use some of the tools I offer in this book, I am not suggesting that they are good role models for those of us interested in engaging in public issues with professional integrity. For one thing, Oreskes and Conway point out that the critics they studied don't play by the same professional rules that the rest of us do. The research they tout to support their alternative view generally does not meet the same peer review standard, in particular.

In many ways, this cynical strategy of casting aside scientific research that has passed peer review and raising up inferior research to replace it—all to create findings that support the public decisions that the critics favor—is an example of the dark side of the engagement force. To add insult to injury, the critics even accuse the mainstream scientists of self-serving behavior and bias, claiming that they simply support each other's claims and publications in order to keep their research funding. Deliberately twisting the way that practicing scientists conduct research into a self-serving cycle is a big threat to the public credibility of all academics and even, I fear, a threat to public support for universities of all kinds, whether public or private.

The power of these ideologically motivated critics of science is evident all over the news. During the 2012 campaign cycle, presidential candidate and then Texas governor Rick Perry offered an opinion on global warming that could have been scripted by Oreskes and Conway's merchants of doubt. Lest you doubt the pervasiveness of this challenge, below I've italicized the phrases that tap into the strategy uncovered by Oreskes and Conway:

> I do believe that the issue of global warming has been politicized. I think there are a *substantial number of scientists who have manipulated data so that they will have dollars rolling into their projects.* And I think we're seeing it almost weekly or even daily, *scientists who are coming forward and questioning the original idea that man-made global warming is what is causing the climate to change.* Yes, our climates change. They've been changing ever since the earth was formed. But I do not buy into, that a group of scientists, who have in

some cases found to be manipulating this information. And the cost to the country and to the world of implementing these anti-carbon programs is in the billions if not trillions of dollars at the end of the day. And *I don't think, from my perspective, that I want America to be engaged in spending that much money on still a scientific theory that has not been proven and from my perspective is more and more being put into question.*[9]

If the debate really isn't about research, then responding as a scholar is not going to be enough for you to escape unscathed. This kind of situation is also exactly why good scientists and scholars need to be better trained to engage with the public. Oreskes and Conway found that many scientists didn't want to get too involved in the public debates that are related to their work. The values of teamwork and consensus, along with the (in my view oddly romantic) belief that truth will win out, all contribute to individual scientists' preference to stay out of the limelight. The cost of obscurity and avoidance is allowing others to dictate the debate and public outcomes, as Oreskes and Conway's work demonstrates. One or two well-known scholars with public followings, like Carl Sagan or Paul Krugman, aren't enough to meet the need for knowledge in the public arena.

In contrast, the cost of engagement is relatively low and tremendously rewarding both in professional terms and in terms of public benefit. The tools of engagement are easy enough to learn and lead to greater effectiveness. The big picture includes not just the scientific questions but also the political context that they fit within. Having a broad professional network puts you in touch with people who might be even better suited than you to deliver your ideas to particular subgroups, such as different faith communities or the communities most adversely affected by a problem you study. Good communications skills allow you to be clear and effective in getting your message heard.

Manage Conflict with Your Network and Communication Skills

The challenge comes in being ready. If you have a sense of what might fuel controversy related to your work on an issue, proceed with an eye on minimizing the material that mischievous outsiders could exploit. The idea behind the suggestions in Box 8.2 is not that you have something to hide, but that you want to avoid allowing someone acting out of a political interest, not scholarly curiosity, to create a perception that your research was somehow inadequate or biased.

Box 8.2. Simple Things You Can Do to Reduce Your Exposure to Conflict

- *Don't assume that your private emails will never be made public.* If you work at a public college or university, your university email account could be subject to a request based on a state open records or freedom of information law (like the Freedom of Information Act, or FOIA, at the federal level). If you are an expert witness in a court case, your emails and other material about the case might be subpoenaed (ask the lawyers you're working with about this).

- *Open a nonuniversity email account.* Use it for any work that might be construed as political or outside normal university business.

- *Know your university's rules about participating in consulting or other outside activities.* If you're a public sector employee, find out about any legal or ethical limitations on your outside work. For example, in Massachusetts, state employees (including professors at UMass) are not allowed to raise money for political campaigns.

Box 8.2. Simple Things You Can Do to Reduce Your Exposure to Conflict (*cont.*)

• *Learn something about FOIA-style requests.*[a] Learning how to gain access to public information is a potentially useful tool in your own research, for one thing. More important, if you're a public employee, then some of your own work might be considered public information, too. Your university counsel is one of the first places to go if you get an open records request.

• *Add a common sense practice to your normal communications: Edit them.* I suspect most of us are already careful about making personal comments about colleagues or professional issues in email messages about campus issues, since it's very easy for one to go astray. Your comments about individuals or organizations should be judicious, and avoid any commentary or back story on your studies that you would not put into a paper or otherwise want to be made public.

• *When you write emails related to your research, also think about how that email might look if taken out of context.* Scientist Phil Jones alluded in an email to a "trick" he used in a paper on global temperature changes. He didn't mean tricking readers into believing something that was wrong, but that's how some suspicious readers of his hacked emails interpreted his use of that word.[b]

• *Extend these email practices to include research-related emails and comments on electronic versions of drafts that you send back and forth with co-authors or reviewers.* Think about how your comments would look from a professional perspective.

• *Destroy or delete drafts and emails that you no longer need.* Law firms have what they call "document retention policies," and that might be useful for some scholars to have, as well. After an article has been published, consider deleting old drafts of the article, comments on previous drafts, and any data that you don't want or don't plan to use again. Empty your sent-email files on a regular basis, and delete work-related emails that you no longer need. Your office and computer will be cleaner, and you'll have less stuff to sift through and explain should someone ever want it.

a The Reporters' Committee for Freedom of the Press has compiled an "Open Government Guide" to state open records laws: http://www.rcfp.org/ogg/index.php.
b Raymond S. Bradley, *Global Warming and Political Intimidation: How Politicians Cracked Down on Scientists as the Earth Heated Up* (Amherst: University of Massachusetts Press, 2011), 146–47.

But let's say your worst fears are realized, and you end up in a situation where you're feeling some unpleasant heat in the public spotlight. Then what? If you've taken this book's advice, you'll also have a team—the network you've carefully cultivated—to back you up and help get you through it.

If you find yourself in a tough spot, don't be afraid to ask for help. Your network can provide many resources for you if and when you need them. The people you know in the political world will be both an early warning system and a source of support should you become somebody's target. The people you know who do public relations for a living can give you advice on how to respond if that becomes necessary. The people you know in the news media will be there to listen and, one hopes, to write intelligently about your take on an issue. Don't be afraid to call on them, and you can even proactively seek advice if you think you're headed into rough waters.

Reworking your communications strategy can also be helpful. You'll still want to think about the message you're conveying, as discussed in the last chapter, but you might need to revise it. Also, carefully rethink your goals for engaging with the media if you're in the middle of a controversy. Colleagues with decades of communication experience have made several useful suggestions about messaging that are in Box 8.3. Chances are you'll never need this advice, but if you do, you'll be ready.

One of the hardest pieces of advice for some scholars to follow through on is figuring out how to stay on message, especially on controversial topics. There are lots of ways to pivot back to your message if someone pulls you in a direction you don't want to go. Psychologist Jennifer Eberhardt studies how unconscious racial biases affect judgments about African Americans by police officers and others. After the 2014 killings of unarmed black men by

> ## Box 8.3. Responding to Controversy about You or Your Research
>
> - Be proactive in getting your message out.
> - Develop your messages carefully. Think about which ones might lead to tangents that take you in a potentially damaging direction and avoid those messages.
> - Don't let the critics of your work or ideas define your message or issue. Reframe the debate if necessary.
> - Stay on message. Remember that when someone asks you a question, you need to respond but not necessarily answer the exact question.
> - Don't engage in hypotheticals if they are posed to you. People in controversies might have healthy imaginations and are likely to twist your intentions and meanings in ways that will not do justice to your argument.

police officers in Ferguson and Staten Island, a journalist asked her about her research: "In Officer Darren Wilson's testimony before the Ferguson, Mo., grand jury, he described Michael Brown as looking 'like a demon.' Is this an example of what you mean?" Eberhardt declined the bait head-on: "I don't want to speak directly on that particular case. I don't know all the details, and maybe we'll never know. However, we have done work in my lab on how African-Americans can be dehumanized in these types of encounters."[10]

You can pivot more subtly, too. Sociologist Amy Schalet's work on teen sexuality generates media questions about controversial issues, such as vaccinating teenagers against HPV. In a television appearance, an interviewer asked her how she would address the concerns of parents who oppose vaccination because it implies permission to have sex. Schalet's answer turned the conversation back to her message about the importance of healthy relationships and communication between parents and teens: "I think what you emphasize is that above all the conversation is important. . . . And that even a conversation about Gardasil can be about, 'This is promoting health. You know, this is something that may eventually become part of your life, sexuality, at a point that you think is healthy, at a point that we hope for you, but we want you to be protected.'"[11]

In addition to how you talk about your message, you should also think carefully about who you talk to during a controversy. If a journalist wants to talk to you, ask yourself what the advantage of talking to them would be before deciding to say yes—even if it's a very high-profile outlet. If they are not presenting the story through a frame you're comfortable with, don't do it. Similarly, consider other audiences you want to reach. An audience with a well-known bias that is unlikely to be persuadable through reason might not be the best choice. But addressing a more ideologically diverse audience, such as a civic group, church group, school, or community organization, might lead to a very productive discussion with a civil and thoughtful exchange of ideas, even if it's heated.

Finally, think hard before participating in formal public debates. Debates implicitly grant equal weight to both sides. If you're asked to debate a topic on which there is little or no legitimate scientific disagreement, such as evolution or global warming, you might be putting yourself in a no-win situation. At the very least, you're likely to run into arguments that you might not be prepared to address, either substantively or rhetorically. I know some scientists who decline to participate in debates about climate change or evolution because they don't want to grant legitimacy to the opposing view. Other public debates are less about science, though. The debate about allowing gay couples to marry has scientific elements but also enough other arguments about norms tied to civic tradition, morality, and religion that a healthy debate can be enlightening (and I, for one, am happy to take part in such events).

Developing a Thicker Skin

The big public controversies are just one end of the conflict spectrum. We are all much more likely to run into conflict situations of some kind when we get immersed in public discussions, and that can also require a little psychological preparation work. Run-of-the-mill disagreements plus the directness of debates in the modern media lead to conflicts that require psychic energy, as we steel ourselves for reactions to our work that we are not used to.

Back in 2008, sociologist Michael Messner was excited to place an op-ed essay in the *Los Angeles Times* advocating that high-income earners pay more in Social Security taxes than they currently did.[12] The reaction to his column stunned him. A flood of email responses included some kudos and some criticism from thoughtful opponents. Most of the responses, though, were nasty enough to send Messner reeling. Those snarky personal emails at first led him to question his ability to be a public intellectual in such an atmosphere, but he eventually decided that to retreat would be to allow the nasty responders to win. Instead, he resolved to thicken his skin and stay in the public debate.

My colleague Nancy Folbre had a similar experience while writing for the *New York Times* Economix blog. Her engagingly written and well-documented posts typically attracted 10,000 hits each week, giving her a great platform to comment on a wide range of economic issues. The first weeks were rough, though. The harsh and hostile comments posted in response to her pieces shocked her. She enlisted some friends to try to keep the comment conversation more civil and on point, but without much success. Eventually, she decided that she was just a sheltered college professor who needed to "get in the game," as she put it.

In both of those situations, venturing into new territory came with some painful lessons about the type of political discourse that new media make possible—very direct, very pointed, and sometimes very personal. While that might be intimidating for some scholars who haven't yet dipped their toe into the sea of engagement, once you're all the way in, you'll get used to the temperature.

The Best Defense: A Strong Ethical Foundation

On a less instrumental level, living by some basic ethical principles can also help you avoid and manage certain kinds of public conflict. Our professions have some ethical rules that we all must live by as scholars—for example, don't make up data and don't plagiarize—and public engagement implies another set of useful ethical norms. Good ethics help you avoid suspicion about your motives and will make you a better researcher-citizen or researcher-activist in the world. Here I assume that you have a public-spirited reason for being publicly engaged, in addition to whatever other motivations you might have.

Recognize your privileged position: Although many of us researchers like to complain about our salaries and workload, it's important to recognize that most established scholars live lives of relative privilege, with an above-average standard of living, a relatively high degree of economic security (at least for those of us with tenure), and some control over our daily schedules. The contrast can be especially stark when we look at the harried, often low-paid activists, organization staff, and public servants that we might work with. We can become easy targets of people who want to stir up conflict in a cauldron of resentment.

Be honest about what you get out of engagement: That unequal positioning of ourselves and those we work with and for can also make us targets for opponents (or even our friends) who might claim that our work and findings serve our self-interest, a la Gov. Rick Perry. And I would agree to an extent that the value of the public-oriented research we do accrues most personally and directly to us. We get data, publications, status, professional experience, paid speaking gigs, teaching material, and grants on top of the financial rewards from our jobs. Sometimes we have the opportunity to get additional pay as a consultant or for summer salary support, and we should assume that someone will want to know that at some point. Yes, we often work long, hard hours for those benefits, but so do the people we work with on our public projects, even when they get nothing extra out of working with us. We should be ready to explain how the value of research for the people we're working with compares with the gains we get.

Share the benefits: Public engagement can present opportunities to share benefits with the organizations and people we work with. Sharing can take many forms beyond the value of the research we produce. Most directly, you can write project budgets that share gains more evenly with other participants who are also making important contributions to the work that you do. Another form of sharing gains might be financial donations back to relevant organizations. Sharing professional gains might also mean co-authoring articles, reports, or op-eds with the people you work with, making sure they are invited to speak to important groups, and treating them generally with the same respect that we give our academic colleagues.

Meet your obligations: Following through with commitments we have made is an ethical imperative in all aspects of professional life, and it's particularly important when working on public issues. People may be counting on you in ways that you cannot see, and there may be a lot at stake related to your research. Also, timeliness matters much more outside of academia. Turning in a scholarly book chapter a month late might not be the end of the world, but missing an opportunity to present research findings at an important public meeting could be very damaging if that's what you were expected to do.

Be the change: In particular, I would argue that those of us whose work addresses social and economic inequalities have an ethical responsibility to "be the change we seek." Our relationships with the people we work with—and for—can be deepened by working thoughtfully and with an eye to our work as a means to reducing inequality, not just an end.

Learning to engage on public issues is not rocket science, thank goodness, although engagement is about doing good science for the public good. Let's take the same high standards that we have for ourselves in the lab, office, library, or field, and learn to use our knowledge and ideas well.

9

Sustainable Engagement
. . . .
How to Stay Productive

When Nicholas Kristof lamented the lack of public engagement among academics in the *New York Times* in 2014, he ignited all of our fears. Is mixing "with the hoi polloi . . . a career killer," as education columnist Rebecca Schuman tweeted? Will this work count in an academic culture with a fair share of snobs? wonders historian and journalist David Perry.[1]

These are deep questions that seem to pose existential trade-offs. If I get involved in public issues, will I still have time to publish in my field so I can get tenure and promotions? If I focus too much on my career, am I selling out my ideals?

How can you, or any busy scholar, add an important effort like public engagement to the long list of family and work demands that you're already juggling without putting your career at risk? It can be done, and it must be done, since to be an effective and engaged scholar, you need to build a successful career as a respected and employed scholar.

One aspect to recognize is that building networks, understanding the big picture, and developing a wide variety of communication skills are not things you do over a weekend or even over a summer break. These are practices that will help you effectively bridge the research world and the rest of the world over the course of your whole career. Issues change, your knowledge evolves, and the state of research shifts over time. Seeing engagement as a developmental process is important for making it sustainable over the long haul, in my opinion.

The arc of Teresa Ghilarducci's career clearly positioned her for influence and effective engagement. Starting with her grad school "apprenticeship in public engagement" as a research assistant working with unions, Ghilarducci made important connections with people who needed practical research. As her knowledge and reputation grew, she made it over the career hurdles of tenure and promotion and built the confidence and expertise to speak plainly but effectively to powerful people.

Would she and other deeply engaged researchers recommend that today's junior scholars get involved in public issues as she did? One paradox I've noticed in talking to people like Ghilarducci is that they would not necessarily recommend plunging into public engagement to junior scholars, recognizing the pressures of the publish-or-perish reward system. On the other hand, they don't seem to regret their own choices, and they have survived and thrived in spite of it! Clearly it is possible to be publicly engaged and yet succeed in academia. The question is how. In addition to patience, successful engagement over the course of a career is made easier by planning to make it sustainable and supportive of career goals *without* making life balance issues worse. This chapter provides some ideas for navigating the most common challenges. No magic formula exists, but in this chapter I pass along some ideas that have worked for others as they balance their professional, personal, and public interests.

Managing Your Time

There are only twenty-four hours in a day for everyone. Economists will tell you the secret formula: It's all about efficiency, that is, getting more done with the time you have. Here are a few efficiency-enhancing tips that will make the time you already spend on professional duties support your efforts to be an effective engaged scholar.

Networking: With an eye on networking as a long-term project, set some short-term goals that are attainable over the next three months, some over the next year, and some others over the next five years. If you have categories of people that you want to connect with, such as newspaper reporters, prominent bloggers, and elected officials, spread your goals across those categories. To make networking more efficient, build it into what you're already doing and make your network grow over time.

- When you travel for a conference or seminar, build in an opportunity to have coffee, a drink, or a short meeting with someone on your list who works in the city where the event is being held. (Or even on a vacation, when you might want a little downtime from your family.) Face time is great for making more lasting connections.
- As you meet with or email with someone you're cultivating for your network, ask them for ideas about others who should be in it. Journalists and advocates will know which policymakers seem especially interested in your research area, and you can probably get the name of the key staff person on that issue.
- In addition to your network map, keep a list somewhere of your contacts that will be easy to edit. People move around but often maintain their professional interest in particular topics. You can use LinkedIn or other social networking sites for keeping all the contact info on

someone. Mainly, though, you just need a simple spreadsheet with names and email addresses, so that you can easily send announcements of new work or other relevant material.

- After your network is fairly well developed, maintaining it is easy and important to do, given changes in the jobs and lives of the folks involved.

Communications: Plan your research projects with an eye to new ways to communicate your findings to new audiences. When you're getting started, imagine who might be interested in your new project and talk to them. As you start publishing your findings, don't call a project finished when you send back corrected galleys. Instead, draft a communications strategy, including a press release and a short blurb to send to your network. Also, shamelessly post that blurb and tweet a link to an article on your research on your blog, Facebook page, and other social networking sites. Once dissemination becomes a habit and you've got the templates and communication skills for this last stage, you'll find that it's easier to do.

Cultivate ties with academic colleagues who do similar work. Those relationships might lead to co-authorship or a sympathetic tenure review in the long run. Those ties have communications value, too, and might also open up opportunities for you to co-author an op-ed piece, for instance, that is more likely to be published as a result of your co-author's ties or location. You can also help each other build policy-relevant questions into your research projects so your work will do double duty—in the same project, you can ask the academically important theory-derived questions *and* learn something that will contribute to public debates.

Efficiency in deploying your new communication skills also means thinking about what the best uses of your time might be. You don't have to—and probably can't—agree to do everything that people ask of you once you are well connected. The time sensitivity of most media opportunities means that you can't take long to decide whether to return a reporter's call on a particular topic and then prepare to talk. If you don't have time to talk (or to gather your wits and come up with a good answer), just call the reporter back and say you're swamped and they should call someone else. Likewise, you can't send a letter to the editor or op-ed in response to every misguided news report you see about your field of study. And you certainly don't have to speak to every group that asks.

Delegation: Teresa Ghilarducci told me her secret to getting research done while also working in the public sphere: "I've got grants, and I have a lot of assistants. I've become very good at project management. . . . At some point in your career that Erik Erikson called your generative moment, you become project managers. That's me."

Ghilarducci put a basic principle to work: One of the most obvious ways to get more done in less time is to have someone else do it for you. Learning to delegate is a standard topic in the business self-help industry, and most scholars could benefit from some tips in this regard as well. The best metaphor I've heard is that delegation is a muscle—you get better by using it, so practice every day.

- Use the resources you have but might not always think about: Your university news office might be able to write or distribute press releases; your departmental staff can send out hard copies of publications and reports if necessary; you can hire a research assistant (RA) to help with many tasks. Undergraduates might be cheaper to hire and can be just as effective as grad students for basic tasks. You can also stretch a small research budget by hiring students who qualify for federal work study funds.
- Set up systems and templates to make it easy to bring in new helpers.

- Choose your RAs wisely. You might want to pick people who have complementary skills to yours, such as organizational ability or experience with nonacademic writing.
- Take the time to train assistants well. Work with them in your office on pieces of projects that you will turn over to them. Think out loud so they better understand what you want them to do. Have them develop flow charts or instructions so you know they're on the right track with the work you give them. Meet with them regularly. Give them constructive feedback. An hour you invest now in training will make them more useful to you later, freeing up many more hours.

General productivity issues: A whole self-help industry caters to busy professionals who think they should be getting more done than they already do. I've found one useful blog, ProfHacker,[2] that reviews time management systems, software, gadgets, and ideas in the context of academia. Although it doesn't deal with the kind of issues described in this book, it might give you some other ideas that will create a little more space in the day for engagement.

Strategies for Enhancing Your Professional Future

You can use your public engagement in ways that will actually enhance your promotability and hireability. You can go farther on what you're doing if you can make your public engagement complementary to your academic life. Don't think about it as a trade-off, where an hour of engagement means one less hour toward tenure. Make that hour work for both goals.

If you're a graduate student, you've probably got the most flexibility, since you most likely have no fixed deadline for completing your program. If you end up spending an extra year because of the engagement work you're doing, no one is likely to notice that year

> **Box 9.1. Using Engagement to Help You Get Tenure and Promotions**
>
> • Be ready to tell your own story of involvement.
> • Collect letters attesting to your valuable work, testimony, or other contributions from nonprofit organizations, community groups, and (especially) powerful people you work with.
> • Cultivate a network of other engaged academics who work on similar topics, and send them your work.
> • Push for additional recognition of the value of engaged scholarship on your campus.

when you go on the job market. Not all of the tips in this section will be relevant for you right away, but your engagement might still help you get a job. For example, drawing on my experiences helping to organize a union in graduate school, I published an article in a labor relations journal. Although my dissertation was on a different labor economics topic, having that article on my CV demonstrated my knowledge of a related area and led to some interesting conversations during job interviews. (In one such conversation, I found a dean of a business school who was a big admirer of the Teamsters!)

If you're a faculty member, particularly one who's pre-tenure, the clock is already ticking toward a tenure or promotion review. The most important part of that review process is documenting your research contributions to your profession. Outside reviewers will read your work and tell your university what they think of you, based on the quality and quantity of your writings. Your history of engagement could help you make a strong case if you do some work along the way and can persuasively use engagement to demonstrate the quality and value of your research.

Be ready to tell your own story of involvement. In many colleges and universities, promotion portfolios include personal statements that allow the faculty member to put his or her work into context. As you weave together a chronological or topical account of your involvement in public issues, the story you tell should tie those activities and accomplishments to the quality of your ideas and research output.

Use those communications skills that you're developing to frame your engagement as scholarship. Here are a few ways you might be able to do that:

- Relate what you learned from working on a public issue to an idea that you had for a research project that you later carried out and published.
- Mention any access to funding or to a pool of potential research subjects that was facilitated by your outreach activities.
- Say what you've learned from the *process* of engagement that's relevant to your field's body of theory, which might be especially relevant for political science, sociology, or history.
- Note any important connections that establish your work as contributing to interdisciplinary goals that your university might have. Does your work have implications for people in other disciplines? Did you work with people in other academic fields in the course of your outreach activities?

Similarly, look for opportunities to frame engagement as teaching. That might be easy if you have involved undergraduates or graduate students in the work you do, and if they got credit or co-authored publications.

Collect letters attesting to your valuable work, testimony, or other contributions from nonprofit organizations, community groups, and (especially) powerful people you work with. If you're doing that work for free, and if it's valuable to them, they will almost certainly agree to do this small favor for you. Ask for these letters right after you've worked with them, while the experience is still fresh in their minds. Address the letter (and deliver a copy) to your department chair. Suggest that the outside person write about the role of your research or your time in some specific activity or issue. Create a folder and keep these letters there for when you need them.

What kinds of powerful people will you know from your network? If you work at a state university, letters from state legislators or other state-level elected officials will surely get some attention. Those individuals help determine the funding fate of our institutions. High-ranking political appointees, like state cabinet secretaries, look good, too. In my own tenure portfolio, I included a personal note from Barney Frank, a member of Congress from our state, thanking me for sending him one of my articles that he'd actually entered into the *Congressional Record* during a floor debate. He had obviously signed the letter—its quirky formatting even made it look like he might have typed it himself.

Build into your network other engaged academics who work on similar topics. Focus on people who are working in the same general area of engagement—those who share interests in your issues or scholarly methods—rather than particular kinds of activities, such as fellow bloggers. Start sending them your academic work and at least some of your nonacademic writings. Ideally, those scholars will be people in your discipline, so they can give you feedback on your academic work, putting them in a good position to be a reviewer for you at tenure or promotion time. They might also open up opportunities for you in your professional organizations that would enhance your standing in your discipline and your prospects for promotion. To meet these colleagues, attend conferences on policy issues that relate to your research, or to research conferences that relate to policy, such as the Association for Public Policy Analysis and Management (APPAM).[3] Go to sessions on public sociology or public anthropology at those professional conferences.

At tenure time, the candidate typically gets to suggest names of reviewers to the committee considering the tenure case. The engaged scholars you're connected to in your own discipline are good options to consider. In some cases, though, you'll be making cross-disciplinary connections. While those scholars might not be as useful as promotion reviewers for your work at some institutions, other universities might still see their comments as valuable if they are close enough. Most promotion committees look for letters from people in universities or colleges that are at a similar or higher status level, so a scholar from a related discipline who has a fancy title and prestigious letterhead might do almost as well as a letter writer in your own field.

The key is to find people who can speak to the scholarly quality of your contributions to the public issue. If you are writing reports for policymakers, they aren't likely to end up in a peer-reviewed journal. But often such reports draw on academic research and apply concepts from our theories and empirical methods. I think it's reasonable to see them as professional writings that make a contribution to scholarship as well as policy, since they broaden our understanding of the world. If you do that kind of work, find someone who can convince a tenure committee to see it as a contribution worthy of credit in your scholarly record. You can also report the number of citations to your report that show up in peer-reviewed articles for additional validation.

I have been asked to make this kind of assessment for people who worked with me as post-doctoral scholars from different disciplines, and it was easy to do in those cases. Here's an edited sample of what I said in one recent case:

Think tank products are sometimes difficult to compare to academic scholarship, and of course the depth varies for such reports. As you can see from the reports described above, the projects that X worked on were substantive and rigorous, making them similar to academic research, in my view. The ABC report is equivalent in rigor and creativity to articles in very good policy journals. The XYZ study used the same rigorous survey and analytical methods found in journal articles. The third report is quite similar to other studies that we have published in law reviews.

The scholars in question got tenure, which was not surprising since they had good records of peer-reviewed publications. Even so, they reported that my assessment of the scholarly quality of work not published in peer-reviewed journals was helpful to their tenure committees in seeing the value of their policy-oriented work.

However, it's important to emphasize that *you* have to take these initiatives, both well before you come up for promotion and during the eventual review process. Tenure committees aren't used to thinking about engaged scholarship in this way. You might also have to help shape your own choices of reviewers to make sure they know how to frame a letter to be convincing.

Push for additional recognition. A longer-term approach to increasing the rewards and professional recognition for public engagement within universities is underway. For instance, the Carnegie Foundation allows universities to apply for a "Community Engagement Elective Classification" that reflects a demonstrated commitment to collaborating with the larger world "for the mutually beneficial exchange of knowledge and resources in a context of partnership and reciprocity."[4] More than 300 colleges and universities have been granted that status by the Carnegie Foundation since 2006. This classification gives faculty a potential mechanism for encouraging more explicit counting of engagement toward hiring, promotion, and tenure.

The application for the Carnegie classification asks for data and policies on faculty involvement in several ways:[5] "Does the institution have search/recruitment policies that encourage the hiring of faculty with expertise in and commitment to community engagement?" "Do the institutional policies for promotion and tenure reward the scholarship of community engagement?" Even when a university receives this recognition, they might not truly use these criteria for faculty personnel decisions. But if it's relevant for your university, it's another point to include in a promotion portfolio.

Remember the Rewards

For many of us, I suspect that the most important motive for engagement is the intrinsic reward of knowing that we've contributed something valuable to an important public debate. Academic blogger Valéria M. Souza goes farther, arguing that concerns about engagement effort as "counting" for professional success miss the point:

> True public engagement is like the voluntary extension of courtesy: you do it not because it "counts" in the sense that you will receive some sort of external reward for it, but because it's both a fundamentally *decent* thing to do and an ethically (or politically) *important* thing to do.[6]

In a somewhat similar vein, Bogenschneider and Corbett suggest that self-rewarding, or defining your own measures of success, can help you develop the patience needed in work in the public realm.[7] Box 9.2 suggests a broad range of markers of "successful" engagement that might help on tough days or in writing up tenure packets.

Box 9.2. What Does Successful Engagement Look Like?

Gaining access to new audiences
- being invited to speak to an influential group of decision makers or voters
- testifying before policymakers
- meeting privately with an influential person or organization
- expanding social media followers

Developing new relationships
- getting to know people in the public sphere who share your commitment
- connecting with other scholars working on the same issue
- creating a formal or informal network of scholars
- making new opportunities for your students
- engaging with members of your community who are working for social change

Leveraging your perspective through the media
- getting an op-ed published and cited in a debate
- having a tweet or blog post reposted or go viral
- being quoted in a news article that connects your work to an issue

Seeing your work used in a debate
- a judge or policymaker cites it in a decision or debate
- someone tells you that your work has changed how they see an issue
- other people cite your work in their own writing or speaking

Seeing movement on an issue that is linked to new knowledge and greater understanding
- a bill is passed or a court decision issued, such as
  - an exclusionary policy is ended, or a new right is recognized
  - new efforts to improve the lives of human beings in education, health care, housing, food security, etc., are enacted and funded
- more resources of attention and funding go to important issues
- positive changes take place in what individuals, organizations, businesses, or public agencies do or don't do
- an issue is reframed in a new and productive way

Box 9.2. What Does Successful Engagement Look Like? (*cont.*)

Being sought after for your knowledge and opinion
- you're asked to do work more targeted to a specific action under consideration
- others consult with you on the implementation or evaluation of a course of action

Enjoying intrinsic rewards
- knowing you've contributed some direct effort for the public good
- being part of social change over the long haul
- acting from your personal ethical values
- doing something for a group of people you care about

If you came to your profession because you wanted to use knowledge in the public interest and to do good, then this chapter probably isn't necessary to convince you of the value of active engagement, but some practical advice might help you turn your idealism into a successful career. The strategies above are designed to allow you to be publicly engaged without hampering your professional progress. Maybe equally importantly, there are other ways that engagement will substantively enhance the quality of your research and teaching and, therefore, your career prospects.

Improving Research

Some scholars get ideas for research from the work they do outside of academia. Daniel A. Smith had conversations with journalists that changed his life: "Little did I know at the time that those two conversations with newsmen—each lasting less than 20 minutes—would inspire my next major research project and ultimately shape the contours of my scholarly career."[8] Smith's public engagement challenged him to ask more relevant questions.

Gary Orfield's book *Congressional Power: Congress and Social Change* came out of his work in the policy arena. "I believe that this book convinced colleagues that I was a true political scientist with something important to say about the central political science questions," Orfield reports. "The lessons I learned from activism gave me the understanding that eventually helped me gain tenure in the discipline."[9]

Many scholars have gotten access to hard-to-obtain data through their engagement. Policymakers and courts can sometimes compel the turning over of data from reluctant sources. Support from policymakers and nonprofit organizations can also be useful in gaining funding, especially when public engagement is an important goal of the funder. The National Science Foundation's requirement to demonstrate "broader impacts" in addition to the intellectual value of a project is a good example.

Finally, being connected to a variety of audiences gives us additional sources of feedback for new projects. For example, John Sides uses blogging to "test-drive" a research project.[10] Bogenschneider and Corbett interviewed a prominent scholar who found that professional relationships with policymakers led her to consider new ideas and ways of framing research.[11]

Better Teaching

Many scholars report that public engagement enhances their teaching. Some of the benefits are very concrete for students: getting better mentors, giving them access to volunteer opportunities, promoting civic virtues, and livening up the classroom with war stories and colorful examples.[12]

Stephanie Coontz is convinced that participating in public discussions with people outside of academia improves her ability to communicate as a teacher and researcher. For example, she has had to reply to people calling in to radio shows with opinions that differ from hers, pushing her to assess the degree of truth in those opinions and grappling with how to communicate her own position better.

The impact of Lisa D. Moore's work on needle exchange programs had lasting effects on her professional life. "For me, work on the needle exchange changed how I think about change and how I teach about change," Moore concludes, looking back on her experience. "When you're young, you think change is kind of linear, binary, and quick. It's kind of like a recipe out there: You add some of this, you add some of that that, and boom you get a cake. . . . People can feel like they've failed when it doesn't work like that. . . . I can teach them so they don't have to be as naïve as I was." She sees this teaching as one of her professional accomplishments: "I've actually mentored a bunch of people to be good change agents."

Creating Additional Value for Universities

Sometimes a university actively encourages faculty to get involved to enhance the institution's image locally or with legislators and donors. Service to your state or your local communities, in particular, will make you popular when politicians want to know what taxpayers' investments in public higher education have generated.

It seems to me that a culture of engagement between researchers and the public is our best tool for winning greater respect and support for science and higher education at every level. Some observers take the concept of engagement a step further, arguing that scientists should even seek elective office to promote the broader interests of science and higher education. Every now and then a scientist gets elected: John Olver, once a faculty member in the University of Massachusetts Amherst Chemistry Department, served our area well as a member of Congress for more than two decades.

Opening Up New Professional Opportunities

Maybe you're thinking, "All this engagement stuff sounds great, but it looks like a full-time job!" You would be correct in the sense that it *could* become a full-time job, which would be a big reward. If you're a social scientist, you could end up doing research for a think tank, a consulting firm, a polling firm, or a politician, and then you really would turn interacting with the public or on public issues into your day job. You could even create your own job by starting an organization that uses research on some issue that you care about if one doesn't already exist, just as Lawrence Lessig did for campaign finance reform. Scholars were behind the start-up of many think tanks.

Just Engage

In my own career, the connections between engagement, research, and teaching have been so closely intertwined that it's hard for me to think about them as creating trade-offs. Each part of that professional triangle presents opportunities for us to learn and create valuable knowledge and materials for conveying that knowledge. Each creates challenges for communicating that knowledge to an audience. Each side of the triangle strengthens our ability to do the others. The practices of engagement outlined in this book are, in many ways, simply extensions of what we ask our students and colleagues—and ourselves—to do at our best inside of academia.

Those of us living the scholarly life often struggle with the challenges of research and teaching, but we don't think of those struggles as a reason to abandon the endeavor. Struggling with how, when, or whether to be a public professor, though, sometimes seems to be a reason to give it up or to put it off.

But somewhere, somebody needs what you know, and they need *you* to be the conduit for that knowledge. The best way to figure out your potential contribution and to explore your own commitment is to jump in. Make that first connection and see where it takes you. Be proactive in building relationships with the people you want to influence.

We all need you to jump in. The people involved in the subject you study need your insights and input. The people who invested in your education (and perhaps your paycheck) need your knowledge to understand their world. Your university colleagues need you to demonstrate the value of having universities. The people in power need your ideas and knowledge to make good decisions, even if they don't know it yet. The people whose lives are affected in good and bad ways by the decisions of others need your efforts to improve their living conditions and opportunities.

We have the potential and opportunity to work with others to make a difference in real peoples' lives. My hope is that this book convinces you of the professional synergies in public engagement as well as of your capacity to add some new activities to your life. Take the next step to being a public professor on the path that will connect you and your research to others so that you can be part of changing the world.

Notes

Chapter 1. Speaking Truth to Empower

1 Story and quotes come from "Gary Orfield: How I Got Started," an interview in the UnBoxed Speaker Series, *YouTube* (December 11, 2008), https://www.youtube.com/watch?v=Mk28WlR-PkI.

2 Gary Orfield, "A Life in Civil Rights," *PS: Political Science & Politics* 43, no. 4 (October 2010), 661.

3 Stories from Teresa Ghilarducci, Stephanie Coontz, and Lisa D. Moore are from interviews with the author.

4 Author's transcription of Dan Quayle's comment in speech to the Commonwealth Club, San Francisco, *YouTube* (May 19, 1992), https://www.youtube.com/watch?v=w8Io65WZnms.

5 Nicholas Kristof, "Professors, We Need You!" *New York Times* (February 16, 2014), http://www.nytimes.com/2014/02/16/opinion/sunday/kristof-professors-we-need-you.html?_r=0 .

6 See, for example, posts to Twitter hashtag #EngagedAcademics. Jesse Daniels compiled a "Round-Up of Kristof's Call for Professors in the Public Sphere," *JustPublics@365* (blog), https://justpublics365.commons.gc.cuny.edu/2014/02/19/roundup-kristof-professors-public-sphere/.

7 Orfield, "A Life in Civil Rights," 666.

Chapter 2. Seeing the Big Picture, Part 1

1 Dave Philipps, "Veteran's Campaign Would Reign in Disability Pay," *New York Times*, (January 8, 2015).

2 Pat Schneider, "Degrees of Risk: UW-Madison's Sara Goldrick-Rab Says College Is a Financial Gamble for Too Many," *Cap Times* (October 29, 2014),

http://host.madison.com/news/local/writers/pat_schneider/degrees-of-risk-uw-madison-s-sara-goldrick-rab-says/article_71710e8a-d792-56ec-afc6-c42405ea933d.html#ixzz3OLB9cdOG.

3 Amanda Little, "A Journalist and a Scientist Break Ground in the G.M.O. Debate," *New Yorker* (April 25, 2014), http://www.newyorker.com/tech/elements/a-journalist-and-a-scientist-break-ground-in-the-g-m-o-debate. The debate can also be viewed at http://vimeo.com/92291215.

4 Jonathan Latham, "Can the Scientific Reputation of Pamela Ronald, Public Face of GMOs, Be Salvaged?" *Independent Science News* (November 12, 2013), http://www.independentsciencenews.org/news/can-the-scientific-reputation-of-pamela-ronald-public-face-of-gmos-be-salvaged/. For an example of a written debate, see *The Economist*'s online debate on biotechnology in 2010: http://www.economist.com/debate/debates/overview/187.

5 The flow chart is based only on data and points made in the debate. All three have also written elsewhere about this issue.

6 That kind of preparation of both sides of the argument is a good idea for anyone, though. Knowing your opponent is one of the first rules of effective competition (a lesson credited to Sun Tzu's *The Art of War*).

7 This description is based on presentations that Aaron Belkin has made and on conversations I have had with him. His book *How We Won: Progressive Lessons from the Repeal of Don't-Ask-Don't-Tell* (Huffington Post Media Group e-book, 2012) documents much of this approach in the context of the gays-in-the-military issue.

8 Vesla Weaver, "High Incarceration May Be More Harmful than High Crime," *Baltimore Sun* (December 21, 2014), http://www.baltimoresun.com/news/opinion/oped/bs-ed-incarceration-rates-20141221-story.html; Jason Stanley and Vesla Weaver, "Is the United States a 'Racial Democracy'?" *New York Times* (January 12, 2014), http://opinionator.blogs.nytimes.com/2014/01/12/is-the-united-states-a-racial-democracy/?_r=1; Amy E. Lerman and Vesla Weaver, "We Should Be Grateful for People Who Take to the Streets," *Slate* (December 23, 2014), http://www.slate.com/articles/news_and_politics/jurisprudence/2014/12/police_brutality_protesters_history_of_civil_rights_women_s_suffrage_child.html.

9 For a summary of the new view, see David Card and Alan B. Krueger, *Myth and Measurement: The New Economics of the Minimum Wage* (Princeton, NJ: Princeton University Press, 1995). A summary of more recent evidence is Arin Dube, Testimony to U.S. Senate Committee on Health, Education, Labor, and Pensions, Hearing on "Keeping Up with a Changing Economy: Indexing the Minimum Wage" (March 14, 2013), http://www.help.senate.gov/imo/media/doc/Dube1.pdf.

10 For an excellent and insightful analysis of the strategic components of policy analysis discussed in this section, see Deborah Stone, *Policy Paradox: The Art of Political Decision Making*, 3rd ed. (New York: Norton, 2012).

11 Teresa Ghilarducci, "Don't Cut Pensions, Expand Them," *New York Times* (March 3, 2012), http://www.nytimes.com/2012/03/16/opinion/pension-funds-for-the-public.html?_r=1&pagewanted=all.

12 Jacob Hacker, "'You Might Be a Public Intellectual If . . .': A Checklist for Political Scientists, a Challenge for Political Science," *PS: Political Science & Politics* 43, no. 4 (October 2010), 657.

Chapter 3. Seeing the Big Picture, Part 2

1 Story reported in Gary Orfield, "A Life in Civil Rights," *PS: Political Science & Politics* 43, no. 4 (October 2010), 665. Statistics are from Judge Meredith's decision: https://www.courtlistener.com/opinion/1582159/liddell-v-bd-of-ed-city-of-st-louis-etc/.

2 National Research Council and Committee on the Use of Social Science Knowledge in Public Policy (Kenneth Prewitt, Thomas A. Schwandt, and Miron L. Straf, eds.), *Using Science as Evidence in Public Policy* (Washington, DC: National Academies Press, 2012), 49.

3 National Conference of State Legislatures, "2014 Minimum Wage Ballot Measures," http://www.ncsl.org/research/labor-and-employment/minimum-wage-ballot-measures.aspx; "State Minimum Wages," http://www.ncsl.org/research/labor-and-employment/state-minimum-wage-chart.aspx.

4 Article 25 of the Universal Declaration of Human Rights: "Everyone has the right to a standard of living adequate for the health and well-being of himself and of his family, including food, clothing, housing and medical care and necessary social services, and the right to security in the event of unemployment, sickness, disability, widowhood, old age or other lack of livelihood in circumstances beyond his control."

5 This list draws on a traditional policy analysis method developed by Eugene Bardach, *A Practical Guide for Policy Analysis: The Eightfold Path to More Effective Problem Solving*, 4th ed. (Thousand Oaks, CA: CQ Press, 2012), and also informed by Deborah Stone's critique of that method in *Policy Paradox: The Art of Political Decision Making,* 3rd ed. (New York: Norton, 2012). The National Research Council report *Using Science as Evidence in Public Policy* suggests a similar role for science in informing public policy.

6 See for example, Thomas Piketty, *Capital in the 21st Century* (Cambridge, MA: Belknap Press, 2014).

7 U.S. Senate Committee on Health, Education, Labor, and Pensions (March 12, 2014), http://www.help.senate.gov/imo/media/doc/Boushey3.pdf.

8   U.S. Senate Committee on Health, Education, Labor, and Pensions (June 25, 2013), http://www.heritage.org/research/testimony/2013/06/ what-is-minimum-wage-its-history-and-effects-on-the-economy.

9   Chris Hellman, presentation at University of Massachusetts Amherst (October 28, 2009).

10 Karen Bogenschneider and Thomas J. Corbett, *Evidence-Based Policymaking* (New York: Routledge, 2010), 25–32.

11 Ibid., 34.

12 Expert Report of William T. Bielby, *Betty Dukes, et al. v. Wal-Mart Stores, Inc.* (February 3, 2003), http://www.walmartclass.com/staticdata/reports/ r3.html.

13 For a more detailed discussion, see Ray LaRaja,and Sidney M. Milkis. "The Honor and Humility of Defending Political Parties in Court," *PS: Political Science & Politics* 37, no. 4 (October 2004), 771–76; and Jonathan S. Krasno and Frank J. Sorauf, "For the Defense," *PS: Political Science & Politics*, 37, no. 4 (October 2004), 777–80.

14 For a description of the process, see Office of Management and Budget, http://www.reginfo.gov/public/reginfo/Regmap/index.jsp.

15 Stephen Greenhouse, "Gap to Raise Minimum Hourly Pay," *New York Times* (February 19, 2014), http://www.nytimes.com/2014/02/20/business/ gap-to-raise-minimum-hourly-pay.html?_r=1.

16 For more information on shareholder activism, see http://ussif.org/projects/ advocacy/resolutions.cfm. For U.S Securities and Exchange Commission regulations about shareholder proposals, see http://ussif.org/projects/ advocacy/resolutions.cfm.

17 Ian Parker, "The Poverty Lab," *New Yorker* (May 17, 2010), 79–89.

18 Sara Goldrick-Rab, "On Scholarly Activism," *Contexts* (blog) (December 4, 2014), contexts.org/blog/on-scholarly-activism/.

19 Andrew Rich, "War of Ideas: Why Mainstream and Liberal Foundations and the Think Tanks They Support Are Losing in the War of Ideas in American Politics," *Stanford Social Innovation Review* (Spring 2004), 18–25.

20 See M. V. Lee Badgett, "Lesbian and Gay Think Tanks: Thinking for Success," in *Identity/Space/Power: Lesbian, Gay, Bisexual, and Transgender Politics*, Mark Blasius, ed. (Princeton, NJ: Princeton University Press, 2000), which draws heavily on James A. Smith, *The Idea Brokers: Think Tanks and the Rise of the New Policy Elite* (New York: Free Press, 1993).

Chapter 4. Effective Networking

1   David Barash, "What If You Wrote a Book and Only One Person Read It?" *Chronicle of Higher Education* (July 12, 2011), http://chronicle.com/blogs/

brainstorm/what-if-you-wrote-a-book-and-only-one-person-read-it/37032?
sid=at&utm_source=at&utm_medium=en.

2 Richard L. Engstrom and Michael P. McDonald, "The Political Scientist as Expert Witness," *PS: Political Science & Politics* 44, no. 2 (April 2011), 285–89.

3 Robert E. Crew, Jr., "The Political Scientist as Local Campaign Consultant," *PS: Political Science & Politics* 44, no. 2 (April 2011), 273–78.

4 John Hird, *Power, Knowledge, and Politics: Policy Analysis in the States* (Washington, DC: Georgetown University Press, 2005), 138–39; Steven R. Nelson, James C. Leffler, and Barbara A. Hansen, "Toward a Research Agenda for Understanding and Improving the Use of Research Evidence" (Portland, OR: Northwest Regional Educational Laboratory, 2009), http://education-northwest.org/sites/default/files/toward-a-research-agenda.pdf; Karen Bogenschneider, and Thomas J. Corbett, *Evidence-Based Policymaking* (New York: Routledge, 2010), 42.

5 A tip for finding email address for someone: google the person's name and an @ sign.

6 Bogenschneider and Corbett, *Evidence-Based Policymaking*, 56.

7 Paul Kix, "Something in the Water," *Boston Globe* (August 21 2011), http://articles.boston.com/2011–08–21/bostonglobe/29912200_1_caleb-banta-green-drug-experts-new-drug.

8 See chapter 7. If you don't use these, the *New York Times*'s David Pogue offers a primer: http://www.nytimes.com/2010/07/08/technology/personaltech/08pogue.html?_r=1&ref=technology&pagewanted=all.

9 Gary Orfield, "A Life in Civil Rights," *PS: Political Science & Politics* 43, no.4 (October 2010), 662.

10 Personal communication (September 13, 2012).

11 Most of the principles here go a long way in the media world, but the institutional contexts and incentives are different.

12 Andra Gillespie and Melissa R. Michelson, "Participant Observation and the Political Scientist: Possibilities, Priorities, and Practicalities," *PS: Political Science & Politics* 44, no. 2 (April 2011), 262.

13 Ibid., 261.

14 See National Research Council and Committee on the Use of Social Science Knowledge in Public Policy (Kenneth Prewitt, Thomas A. Schwandt, and Miron L. Straf, eds.), *Using Science as Evidence in Public Policy* (Washington, DC: National Academies Press, 2012); Bogenschneider, and Corbett, *Evidence-Based Policymaking*.

15 Bogenschneider and Corbett, *Evidence-Based Policymaking*, 191.

16 Orfield, "A Life in Civil Rights," 664.

Chapter 5. Communicating outside of the Academy

1 Carrie Baker, "Jailing Girls for Men's Crimes," *Ms. Magazine Blog*, http://msmagazine.com/blog/blog/2010/12/08/jailing-girls-for-mens-crimes/. Baker's story is based on personal communication and on Lauren Sieben, "Scholar Who Studies Sex Trafficking Wins National Journalism Award," *Chronicle of Higher Education* (May 1, 2011). Following Baker quotes are from Sieben's article.

2 Amitai Etzioni, "Reflections of a Sometimes Public Intellectual," *PS: Political Science & Politics* 43, no. 4 (October 2010), 651.

3 Michael Warner, "Media Gays: A New Stonewall," *Nation* (July 14, 1997), 15–19.

4 Judith Butler, "A 'Bad Writer' Bites Back," *New York Times* (March 20, 1999), http://query.nytimes.com/gst/fullpage.html?res=950CE5D61531F933A15750C0A96F958260&scp=4&sq=%22judith%20butler%22&st=cse.

5 See June Cohen's talk, "What Makes a Great TED Talk?" (September 29, 2010), https://www.youtube.com/watch?v=RVDfWfUSBIM&feature=kp.

6 Etzioni, "Reflections of a Sometimes Public Intellectual," 651.

7 This is a rephrasing of a question in the introduction of this report: Robert Pollin, Heidi Garrett-Peltier, James Heintz, and Bracken Hendricks, "Green Growth: A U.S. Program for Controlling Climate Change and Expanding Job Opportunities" (Washington, DC: Center for American Progress, September 2014), 2, http://cdn.americanprogress.org/wp-content/uploads/2014/09/GreenGrowth-SUMMARY.pdf.

8 Aaron Belkin, *How We Won: Progressive Lessons from the Repeal of Don't-Ask-Don't-Tell* (Huffington Post Media Group e-book, 2012), 20.

9 Raymond S. Bradley, *Global Warming and Political Intimidation: How Politicians Cracked Down on Scientists as the Earth Heated Up* (Amherst: University of Massachusetts Press, 2011); Intergovernmental Panel on Climate Change, *Climate Change 2014: Synthesis Report*, Summary for Policymakers, http://www.ipcc.ch/pdf/assessment-report/ar5/syr/SYR_AR5_SPMcorr1.pdf.

10 Pollin et al., "Green Growth."

11 Robert Jensen, *Writing Dissent: Taking Radical Ideas from the Margins to the Mainstream* (New York: Peter Lang 2001).

12 As your network expands, you're likely to add people in organizations who do messaging research or are consumers of such research. You won't typically find the results of that messaging research per se on an organization's website, but you will find the messages that they think work. As you get to know them better, ask about the polling to better understand why they frame issues as they do, and you can try out your own ideas.

13 George Lakoff, *Don't Think of an Elephant: Know Your Values and Frame the Debate* (White River Junction, VT: Chelsea Green Publishing, 2004), xv.

14 Ibid., 17.

15 Luntz Research Companies, "Straight Talk" (n.d.), 133, https://www2.bc.edu/~plater/Newpublicsite06/suppmats/02.6.pdf.

16 Saul Alinksy, *Rules for Radicals* (New York: Random House 1971), 81, http://servv89pn0aj.sn.sourcedns.com/~gbpprorg/obama/Rules_for_Radicals.pdf.

17 Lakoff, *Don't Think of an Elephant*, xv.

18 Deborah Stone, *Policy Paradox: The Art of Political Decision Making*, 3rd ed. (New York: Norton, 2012).

19 See William Rubenstein "Do Gay Rights Laws Matter?: An Empirical Assessment," *Southern California Law Review* 75 (2001), 65–120. Also see update by Christopher Ramos, M. V. Lee Badgett, and Brad Sears, "Evidence of Employment Discrimination on the Basis of Sexual Orientation and Gender Identity: Complaints Filed with State Enforcement Agencies, 1999–2007" (Los Angeles: Williams Institute, 2008), http://williamsinstitute.law.ucla.edu/wp-content/uploads/Badgett-Sears-Ramos-Emply-Discrim-1999–2007-Nov-08.pdf.

20 See the Cultural Cognition Project's website for related studies: http://www.culturalcognition.net/. This discussion is largely based on Dan M. Kahan, Donald Braman, Paul Slovic, John Gastil, and Geoffrey Cohen, "The Second National Risk and Culture Study: Making Sense of—and Making Progress In—the American Culture War of Fact" (New Haven, CT: Cultural Cognition Project at Yale Law School, 2007), http://papers.ssrn.com/sol3/papers.cfm?abstract_id=1017189.

21 Cultural Cognition Project, Yale Law School, "The Cultural Cognition of Gay and Lesbian Parenting: Summary of First Round Data Collection" (n.d.), http://www.culturalcognition.net/storage/Stage%201%20Report.pdf.

22 Kahan et al., "The Second National Risk and Culture Study."

23 Belkin, *How We Won*, 29.

Chapter 6. Using Traditional Media Outlets to Connect with the World

1 Amy T. Schalet, *Not under My Roof: Parents, Teens and the Culture of Sex* (Chicago: University of Chicago Press, 2011).

2 See Karen Bogenschneider and Thomas J. Corbett, *Evidence-Based Policymaking* (New York: Routledge, 2010), 45–48.

3 Kimberlee Weaver, Stephen M. Garcia, Norbert Schwarz, and Dale T. Miller, "Inferring the Popularity of an Opinion From Its Familiarity: A Repetitive Voice Can Sound Like a Chorus," *Journal of Personality and Social Psychology*

92, no. 5 (2007), 821–33. Also Ian Skurnik, Carolyn Yoon, Denise C. Park, and Norbert Schwarz, "How Warnings about False Claims Become Recommendations," *Journal of Consumer Research* 31, no. 4 (2005), 713–24.

4 Glenda M. Russell, "Surviving and Thriving in the Midst of Anti-Gay Politics," *Angles* 7, no. 2 (2004), 1–8.

5 Amy T. Schalet, "The New ABCD's of Talking about Sex with Teenagers," *Huffington Post* (November 2, 2011), http://www.huffingtonpost.com/amy-schalet/teenagers-sex-talk_b_1072504.html.

6 See Bogenschneider and Corbett, *Evidence-Based Policymaking*, 53.

7 Robert Jensen, *Writing Dissent: Taking Radical Ideas from the Margins to the Mainstream* (New York: Peter Lang, 2005), 103–6.

8 Tim Donnelly, "How to Write a Press Release," *Inc.* (September 3, 2010), http://www.inc.com/guides/2010/09/how-to-write-a-press-release.html.

9 Many thanks to Cathy Renna, Michael Lavers, and Peter Montgomery for sharing their insights and tips for television that I use in this section and Box 6.6.

10 Jensen, *Writing Dissent*, 36.

11 You can see others that we've gathered at UMass: www.umass.edu/pep/.

Chapter 7. Using Social Media to Connect with the World

1 On February 15, 2015, Sociological Images had more than 70,000 followers on Facebook and 14,000 on Pinterest, and Twitter name @socimages had 21,900 followers.

2 Scott B. Swenson is vice president and director of communications for Common Cause. He also directed the Piper Fund's Communication Collaborative on Money in Politics at ReThink Media, and was director of legislative and strategic communications at the ACLU and executive editor of RH Reality Check.

3 From May 1 through July 4, 2014, Lessig raised more than $5 million, according to his blog posts: http://lessig.tumblr.com/. By February 2015, Mayday had raised more than $11 million from over 68,000 individual contributors; see https://mayday.us/about_us/ (accessed February 20, 2015).

4 For Facebook, see Wikipedia entry: http://en.wikipedia.org/wiki/Facebook. For Twitter ("288 million monthly active users") figures, see the company's website: about.twitter.com/company (accessed April 6, 2015).

5 Most academic journals have copyright issues with posting an article publicly, but at the very least most will allow you to post a copy of the last draft in manuscript form.

6 This figure comes from Pew Research (June 14, 2014), http://www.pewresearch.org/fact-tank/2014/02/03/6-new-facts-about-facebook/.

7 Ibid.

8   Here's Raul Pacheco-Vega's description of these hashtags: http://www.
    raulpacheco.org/2012/09/scholarsunday/, and http://www.raulpacheco.
    org/2012/01/knowledge-translation-mobilization-and-the-myresearch-
    hashtag/?utm_content=buffer207db&utm_medium=social&utm_
    source=twitter.com&utm_campaign=buffer.

9   Alicia Garza, "A Herstory of the #BlackLivesMatter Movement," *Feminist Wire*
    (October 7, 2014), http://thefeministwire.com/2014/10/blacklivesmatter-2/;
    Jay Caspian Kang, "'Our Demand Is Simple: Stop Killing Us,'" *New York Times
    Magazine* (May 4, 2015), http://www.nytimes.com/2015/05/10/magazine/
    our-demand-is-simple-stop-killing-us.html?_r=0.

10 Feminista Jones, "Is Twitter the Underground Railroad of Activism?" *Salon*
    (July 17, 2013), http://www.salon.com/2013/07/17/how_twitter_fuels_black_
    activism/; Sofia Ballin, "In Black Twitter, Giving Voice and Driving the
    Debate," *Philly.com* (January 22, 2015), http://articles.philly.com/2015–
    01–22/entertainment/58349170_1_revlon-black-protests-ferguson.

11 Wolfers told this story at a conference session at the Allied Social Science
    Association Meetings for economists (January 3, 2015).

12 See Justin Wolfers, https://twitter.com/JustinWolfers/
    status/335017341295419394.

13 Dan Zarrella, "New Data Proves 'Please ReTweet' Generates 4x More
    ReTweets [Data]," *HubSpot Blogs* (May 31, 2011), https://blog.hubspot.com/
    blog/tabid/6307/bid/14982/New-Data-Proves-Please-ReTweet-Generates-
    4x-More-ReTweets-Data.aspx.

14 John Sides, "The Political Scientist as Blogger," *PS: Political Science & Politics*
    44, no. 2 (April 2011), 267.

15 Ibid., 269.

16 Ibid., 270.

17 Amitai Etzioni, "Reflections of a Sometimes Public Intellectual," *PS: Political
    Science & Politics* 43, no. 4 (October 2010), 652.

18 Clair Cain Miller, "The Plus in Google Plus? It's Mostly for Google," *New York
    Times* (February 14, 2014), http://www.nytimes.com/2014/02/15/technol-
    ogy/the-plus-in-google-plus-its-mostly-for-google.html?_r=0.

Chapter 8. In the Heat of the Moment

1   Jonathan Cohn, "What Jon Gruber's Quotes Really Tell Us about
    Obamacare—and American Politics," *New Republic* (November 17, 2014),
    http://www.newrepublic.com/article/120311/jonathan-gruber-and-obamacare-
    what-his-quotes-really-tell-us.

2   David Nather, "Will Jonathan Gruber Bring Down Obamacare?" *Politico
    Magazine* (December 7, 2014), http://www.politico.com/magazine/

story/2014/12/will-jonathan-gruber-topple-obamacare-113369.html#.
VOJpjrDF_3J.

3 Robert Pear, "Jonathan Gruber of M.I.T. Regrets 'Arrogance' on Health Law,"
New York Times (December 9, 2014), http://www.nytimes.com/2014/12/10/
us/jonathan-gruber-of-mit-regrets-arrogance-on-health-law.html.

4 See, for example, David Card and Alan B. Krueger, *Myth and Measurement:
The New Economics of the Minimum Wage* (Princeton, NJ: Princeton
University Press 1995).

5 Quoted in Douglas Clement, "Interview with David Card," *Banking and Policy
Issues Magazine* (December 2006), http://www.minneapolisfed.org/
publications_papers/pub_display.cfm?id=3190.

6 Ibid.

7 Michael Luo, "N.R.A. Stymies Firearms Research, Scientists Say," *New York
Times* (January 25, 2011), http://www.nytimes.com/2011/01/26/us/26guns.
html?_r=1&scp=3&sq=research%20gun%20control&st=cse.

8 Naomi Oreskes and Erik M. Conway, *Merchants of Doubt* (New York:
Bloomsbury Press, 2010), 42.

9 The statement was widely reported, and this is my transcription from
Associated Press, "Perry Doubts Manmade Global Warming," *YouTube*
(August 17, 2011), https://www.youtube.com/watch?v=tZozN-zhku4. Part of
the quote is included on the *Washington Post*'s Fact Checker webpage: Glenn
Kessler, "Rick Perry's Made-Up 'Facts' about Climate Change," *Washington
Post* (August 18, 2011),http://www.washingtonpost.com/blogs/fact-checker/
post/rick-perrys-made-up-facts-about-climate-change/2011/08/17/gIQApV-
F5LJ_blog.html?hpid=z1. According to Kessler's analysis, there is no good
evidence backing any of these assertions by Perry. See also Raymond S.
Bradley, *Global Warming and Political Intimidation: How Politicians Cracked
Down on Scientists as the Earth Heated Up* (Amherst: University of
Massachusetts Press, 2011), which provides more background and analysis of
the large body of scientific evidence refuting Perry's argument.

10 Exchange in Claudia Dreyfus, "Perceptions of Race at a Glance," *New York
Times* (January 5, 2015), http://www.nytimes.com/2015/01/06/science/a--
macarthur-grant-winner-tries-to-unearth-biases-to-aid-criminal-justice.html?
rref=collection%2Fcolumn%2Fa-conversation-with.

11 *CNN American Morning* (December 26, 2011), http://am.blogs.cnn.
com/2011/12/26/do-teen-sleepovers-prevent-pregnancy-one-researcher-
says-yes-and-explains-why/.

12 Michael Messner, "One 'Bonus' We Don't Need," *Los Angeles Times*
(December 9, 2008), http://articles.latimes.com/2008/dec/09/opinion/
oe-messner9; Messner wrote about the aftermath in "A Public Intellectual

Feels the Heat," *Chronicle of Higher Education* (April 11, 2010), http://chronicle.com/article/A-Public-Intellectual-Feels/64986/?key=Hml6dVJgOS JEbHUxfSlMfioFYXUuIEh5bXVEYXAaYllW.

Chapter 9. Sustainable Engagement

1 David Perry, "Academics in Public," *How Did We Get into This Mess?* (blog) (February 18, 2014), http://www.thismess.net/2014/02/academics-in-public-belated-response-to.html.

2 *ProfHacker* blog, *Chronicle of Higher Education*, http://chronicle.com/blogs/profhacker/.

3 Karen Bogenschneider and Thomas J. Corbett, *Evidence-Based Policymaking* (New York: Routledge, 2010), 201.

4 Carnegie Foundation, http://classifications.carnegiefoundation.org/descriptions/community_engagement.php?key=1213.

5 These quotes come from the 2010 application: http://classifications.carnegiefoundation.org/downloads/2010-Documentation-Reporting-Form-PREVIEW-v2.pdf.

6 Valeria Souza, "You're Doing It Wrong," *It's Complicated* (blog) (February 22, 2014), http://valeriamsouza.wordpress.com/2014/02/22/public-engagement-youre-doing-it-wrong/.

7 Bogenschneider and Corbett, *Evidence-Based Policymaking*.

8 Daniel A. Smith, "Generating Scholarship from Public Service: Media Outreach, Nonprofit Foundation Service, and Legal Expert Consulting," *PS: Political Science & Politics* 44, no. 2 (April 2011), 256.

9 Gary Orfield, "A Life in Civil Rights," *PS: Political Science & Politics* 43, no. 4 (October 2010), 661–70.

10 John Sides, "The Political Scientist as Blogger," *PS: Political Science & Politics* 44, no. 2 (April 2011), 267–71.

11 Bogenschneider and Corbett, *Evidence-Based Policymaking*, 198.

12 See Ann Marie Murphy and Andreas Fulda, "Bridging the Gap: Pracademics in Foreign Policy," *PS: Political Science & Politics* 44, no. 2 (April 2011), 279–83; Richard L. Engstrom and Michael P. McDonald, "The Political Scientist as Expert Witness," *PS: Political Science & Politics* 44, no. 2 (April 2011), 285–89; Robert E Crew, Jr., "The Political Scientist as Local Campaign Consultant," *PS: Political Science & Politics* 44, no. 2 (April 2011), 273–78; Smith, "Generating Scholarship from Public Service."

Index

About the Author

M. V. Lee Badgett has twenty-five years of experience connecting cutting-edge research with the policy and community locations that need those findings. She is Professor of Economics and Director of the Center for Public Policy and Administration at the University of Massachusetts–Amherst. She is also Williams Distinguished Scholar at UCLA's Williams Institute. Her publications include *When Gay People Get Married: What Happens When Societies Legalize Same-Sex Marriage* and *Money, Myths, and Change: The Economic Lives of Lesbians and Gay Men.*